To ~~Peggy~~

From ~~Dalton~~.

Wishing you a Happy Birthday.

June 6/28

The Princess Elizabeth, Heir Presumptive, who may some day be Queen

THE PRINCESS ELIZABETH

The Princess Elizabeth

CAPTAIN
ERIC ACLAND
Author of
The House of Windsor
Long Live the King, etc.

The John C. Winston Co., Limited
Toronto

Princess Elizabeth

Printed in Canada

To Elizabeth Anne Acland, our tiny
daughter, and to all good little
people of the Empire over
which H.R.H. Elizabeth of
York, will some day rule,
this story is especially
dedicated.

FOREWORD

All children, the world over, love the story of a little princess and because this is a story of a dear little girl who is destined to become the greatest ruler in Christendom, her life and training is perhaps the greatest children's story of all time.

I would remind all parents of the tribulations and the sorrow which the British Royal family has passed through. Like the Throne itself, the Royal Family has emerged from this valley of shadows into the warm sunlight that is the love and respect of all peoples of the Empire.

I think the main reason for this is that the Royal Family raised by King George V and Queen Mary had given each one of its members the fundamental foundation upon which a Christian gentleman and gentlewoman is built.

The task of training and fitting The Princess Elizabeth for the lifelong duty that she faces did not commence on the fateful day when her uncle abdicated the Throne. It began as far back as her cradle days. Again, in this, the House of Windsor has not been found wanting. Therefore, good parents, I do not hesitate to give your children this storybook saga of the life of The Princess Elizabeth of York. It is my hope that they will enjoy it as much as did little Anne Acland.

—THE AUTHOR

CONTENTS

CONTENTS

I

A PRINCESS IS BORN

THIS is the story of a real, live princess—of a charming little girl with dancing blue eyes and a coronet of golden hair who will probably some day rule over the greatest Empire the world has ever known.

You may search the storybooks until the type goes whirling round before your eyes, but no fairy princess will you find with a more glorious future or a more romantic past than that of The Princess Elizabeth of York, whose father is now King-Emperor and whose mother is Queen.

This Empire encircles the world. It stretches from the barren lands of the Arctic, where Canada has dominion over the land of the midnight sun, to the rich Indian Empire, where more people live than in the whole of America and Europe put together. It has truly been said that the sun never sets on the British Empire. Some day this Princess will be ruler of this vast Empire. People of hundreds of races and creeds pray that she may be their Queen-

Empress, for they remember another Princess Elizabeth who became a very great Queen indeed.

It was over four hundred years ago, when England was a tiny country and this Empire unheard of, that the little Princess Elizabeth who was to become Good Queen Bess was born. That was a hundred years before the Pilgrim Fathers sailed in the *Mayflower* and before there was any permanent English settlement in America.

Sailors and soldiers, explorers and writers all mustered to serve this Queen, and in her service laid the foundation for the British Empire as we know it today.

Even though they had only small ships and had to defeat single-handed the Armada of the mighty Empire of Spain, there was something about this great Queen of England that made men fight against desperate odds, something that made men fearless, willing to brave dark and unknown seas in tiny ships and able to found the mighty Empire, in the name of Elizabeth of England.

This Princess Elizabeth, who was the daughter of King Henry VIII, was born in the favourite home of English Kings in those days, Greenwich Palace. But The Princess Elizabeth of York, about whom this story is written, was not born in a palace of gold or even in a great mansion, for her father was the second son of the King and her mother was not a princess, but a charming Scottish lady.

The Princess Elizabeth of our story was born at 17, Bruton Street in old London, a very dignified but quite ordinary town house like hundreds of others. It was very early on the morning of April 21, 1926, that The Princess Elizabeth first arrived at the Bruton Street home. As you know, London is very cold and damp in the springtime. But in spite of all the rain, hundreds and hundreds of people stayed outside the house with the little iron railing all night long, hoping that they might be the first to hear the glad tidings. Good-humoured policemen, rocking backwards and forwards on their heels, were asked over and over again, "Is it a Prince or a Princess?"

It was three o'clock in the morning before they were able to answer. "It's a baby girl, a Princess." They beamed until the chin straps on their helmets all but cracked. By then, the news had gone out from Bruton Street to the whole Empire as crackling wireless relayed the message to the far corners of the earth. Newsboys in Capetown, Toronto, and Calcutta were soon shouting: "A Princess is born to the Duke and Duchess of York!"

With the first glimmer of the grey London dawn, motor cars began to arrive. The first was a Government car. Its passenger mounted the steps to the front door, three at a time, as if his short legs could not possibly get him inside fast enough. He was the Home Secretary Sir William Joynson-Hicks. When a little British Princess first bows to the world, this officer of the Government must first greet her, for that is the traditional wish of the people.

The Home Secretary, his puckered face the more puckered with smiles, congratulates the tall, handsome Duke who has this very morning become a father. Later, stepping from step to step very gingerly, as if he might awaken—he knew not what —in this magic house, Sir William climbs to the floor above.

Quietly, on tiptoe, the Home Secretary approaches the baby Princess, a precious mite bundled in white. He bows respectfully and rightly so, for it is indeed a great honour to welcome this little Princess into the world!

The baby Princess opens her eyes and stares, as all babies will, at the strange gentleman. She yawns, thereby ending her first audience, closes her eyes, and falls fast asleep!

One of the next cars to arrive bears the Royal Standard. "It's the Queen!" shouts someone at the edge of the crowd, and it is, indeed, the Queen.

As she steps to the pavement, all the men sweep their hats from their heads. Everyone in the crowd smiles and Her Majesty smiles back as she walks to the door, for everyone loves a grandmother and likes to share her happiness on such a day.

The Queen is delighted with the baby Princess. Her Majesty smiles over the cradle. "What a good baby! I do hope you are like your little mother!"

The Countess of Strathmore, the baby's other grandmother; her Royal uncles, the Princes, Edward of Wales; Henry, Duke of Gloucester; George, Duke of Kent; and her aunt, Princess Mary, are all soon to gather at the baby Princess's first Court at Bruton Street—not in a palace royal but in a rented home. This house was later used as an office by men of the Canadian Pacific Railway.

II

THREE GLORIOUS NAMES

ELIZABETH, Alexandra, Mary, were the beautiful names chosen for this baby Princess of York as she rested in the arms of her nurse in the large bedroom set apart for her on the top floor of the Bruton Street house. ˙

Elizabeth of York!   The small, fair, curly head that peeked out from a bundle of shawls, as her nurse carried her on her first "walks" around old Berkeley Square under the fresh budding trees, did not as yet know that England's greatest name was hers to have and to hold for life.

It was nice that they called this little baby Princess after her mother for she had already won the hearts of the people as the Duchess of York.   Yet, as the good King her grandfather pointed out when all the Royal relatives were ˉselecting her names, this was surely the wisest and most glorious choice.

So it was that, on a bright spring day, the baby Princess wrapped in shawls and cooing with happiness was carried out of her father's house by her

The infant Princess Elizabeth and her mother

nurse, and with her mother was driven to Buckingham Palace where the Royal Family waited the hour of her christening.

In the private chapel of the King they gave the little Princess those three great names—Elizabeth, after her Scottish mother, and mindful of the mighty power it brought from far-off days in England's history; Alexandra, after her great-grandmother Queen Alexandra, mother of the King; and Mary, a beautiful name that her grandmother had made even more beautiful before the eyes of the King's subjects.

Before the baby Princess was carried into the chapel, a wondrous robe was wrapped about her. It was of rich, ivory lace from Brussels and very old. Princess Victoria, who became the Good Queen, had worn it when she was christened four years after the Battle of Waterloo and more than fifty years before Canada became a Dominion. Since that time it has been worn by each heir to the throne at his own christening.

The Chapel Royal, where the Kings of England worship before their God, was filled with sweet fragrance this day for it had been especially decorated with crimson and white flowers. It was the Archbishop of York, wearing the gold-encrusted vestments of the Church of England, who traced the

2

figure of the Cross upon the head of the infant Princess. Long before there had been Princesses of York or even Kings of Great Britain, the Church of England had been established. And so, because the State recognizes it as the national church of the English people and because it plays an important part in the constitution of the realm, primates of the Church of England always take part in such ceremonies.

Two high ministers of the church, who hold the rank of Lords Spiritual and are permitted to sit in the House of Lords, always officiate at ceremonies having to do with the Royal Family. These are the Archbishop of Canterbury, the primate of all England and who in the table of precedence is senior to the Prime Minister and follows only after the Royal Family in rank, and the Archbishop of York who follows the Lord Chancellor in precedence or position. The Archbishop of Canterbury always crowns the King at a coronation and the Archbishop of York, the Queen.

So it was that the Archbishop of York christened the baby The Princess Elizabeth and he did so with water from the Royal gold font, water that had been brought all the way from the River Jordan for the occasion.

After the Royal Family left the chapel, they all went to The Princess Elizabeth's first tea party, given by her father and mother, the Duke and Duchess of York. It was a wonderful tea party. The King and Queen, as proud a grandfather and grandmother as lived in the realm that day, along with the three Princes who were her uncles, and her grandparents from Scotland, talked gaily of what the future days would bring to The Princess Elizabeth of York.

But by far the most gorgeous thing at her first tea party, was the pretty christening cake that her mother cut. It was certainly lovely, with little silver figures standing clear of the icing and crowning the cake in the form of a beautiful cradle of silver, and in the cradle, a tiny baby doll.

Then, back to the nursery at Bruton Street the babe was taken from the great gold and silver palace of the King and Queen.

In this nursery, where the windows looked over the roof tops of old London and out onto Grafton Street, the little Princess kicked her legs under the coverlets of her white cot that glistened in the firelight. To her came many visitors and friends.

"Yes, she has gorgeous, big, blue eyes, and the whitest skin in the world, and when she smiles—well, it is just like a cherub smiling from a cloud of whiteness," they said.

She cried, of course, as all healthy babies will, but, "She seems to like to smile and laugh and curl

her toes, and she hardly cries at all," said a Great
Lady.

And so the first news of the most wonderful baby
in the land went out bit by bit to her grandfather's
loyal subjects, while she cooed and laughed by the
fireside.

III

A CARGO OF TOYS

THREE months later, The Princess Elizabeth of York went on her first long train journey. The journey in itself was an adventure, for few little ladies of three months are in the habit of travelling from London to Scotland by train. But the Princess comes of a Royal Family of travellers, for her uncle, the Prince of Wales, at that time had already earned the reputation of being the most travelled young man in the whole Empire. So the baby girl suffered her long trip as if she were the most experienced traveller in the whole world. She slept during most of the trip. But now and again she awoke to watch the green summer countryside go slipping past as the express roared its way northward to the Highlands of Scotland.

It was the Princess's first visit to the ancestral castle home of her Scottish grandfather and grandmother, the Earl and Countess of Strathmore. These grandparents were in their own right the descendants of the Scottish kings of old. Glamis

Castle, in the County of Forfarshire, was her mother's home. It was here that the Duchess, as the Lady Elizabeth Bowes-Lyon, had grown to girlhood, surrounded by the princely traditions of the Highland chieftains.

The castle, for all its cold grey ramparts and towers—and we shall tell you more about them later—welcomed the little Princess as one of its very own, and Highland folk from all the countryside adopted her in their hearts.

Baby Elizabeth thrived and grew straight of limb during her first stay at historic old Glamis Castle. On sunny days she slept under the trees amid the flowers of the castle grounds, or watched her father play tennis on the courts or saw him start out for a day's fishing or shooting, after a farewell kiss on the forehead of his little daughter.

But the baby, so happy with her grandparents and her father and mother, was all too soon to feel the shadow of duty that must come to all those of Royal birth.

Although the little Princess cannot remember much about it all, her first Christmas at Sandringham was a happy one. Her father and mother, however, knew that in a few short weeks they would be sailing the seas for the other side of the world, each turn of the war-ship's propellers taking them farther and farther away from the little girl they loved so dearly. But this must be, for her father, the Duke of York, and her mother, the Duchess, were expected to open the beautiful new Houses of Parliament at Canberra, the capital of Australia.

Before the Duchess of York sailed away early in January, she fondly placed about the neck of little Elizabeth the Princess's first gift of jewellery, a simple string of coral beads. And they did bring good luck! They not only brought good luck to the baby and to her father and mother who came safely home, but to a thousand and one jewellers all through the land. For when it became known that The Princess Elizabeth's mother had given her coral beads, other mothers throughout the land brought coral beads to give to their own little girls!

For the next six months, Elizabeth divided her time, living for three months in the Royal Nursery at Buckingham Palace, and three months with her Scottish grandparents. Each and every day during her stay at the Royal Palace, the Princess, seated on a special silken cushion, would have tea with her grandmother the Queen. It was the first of a thousand happy tea parties with Grandmother.

At last came the great day, the day that the baby princess had so long waited for. Mummy and Daddy were coming back! Rosy with excitement and wearing her very best frock, she waited with Grandmother for the door to open. There they were at last!

"Mummy! Daddy!" shrieked Elizabeth, flinging out her two chubby little arms. It was indeed a grand reunion.

These were her first two words, though her good grandfather, the King, smiling in his beard, chided her father and mother by telling them that these were the first words—*after* "Grandpa."

Outside Buckingham Palace, tens of thousands of the people of London had greeted the Duke and Duchess upon their return. Now they were calling for their Princess!

In the arms of her mother, with her father standing by, Elizabeth was carried to the balcony where she first looked down upon a vast throng of her grandfather's loyal subjects. A mighty cheer went up as the people saw the little Princess with her Royal father and mother.

Elizabeth of York, now a golden-haired little girl of fourteen months, waved her hand. It was the happiest day she had yet had, for Mummy and Daddy had come home to stay.

Back with them in the mighty battle cruiser *Renown*, the Royal father and mother had brought from the people on the other side of the world a

cargo of presents for Elizabeth such as no other
little girl in this world has ever had sent her before.
Teddy Bears by the hundreds, toy soldiers, rattles,
twenty-five real live parrots, twittering canaries,
miniature chairs and tables, gollywogs that talked
and gollywogs that walked; three tons of toys, of
every size and colour and kind! You see, the people
in far-off Australia already loved this child who was,
they said, "Our Princess of York."

While the tiny Princess was enjoying golden
moments of reunion, giant winches were bringing
treasures up from the vast hold of the battleship
Renown. Treasures in toys that no fairy princess
could have dreamed of in the far-off ages.

"Lumme, 'er 'Ighness will have a time undoing
these parcels," muttered a seaman to a fellow blue-
jacket as the two guided a great packing case clear
of the hatchway. The packing case was as big as a
gun turret and was crowded with giant Teddy Bears.

But the old sailor was wrong, for the little Princess
saw but few of those wondrous toys. Princesses, like
all other little girls, can have too many toys. Besides,
there were thousands of poor children in England
who had never owned a Teddy Bear. So The Princess Elizabeth sent them to children in hospitals and
children in poor homes. Her first ambassadors,
they were, these funny gollywogs and Teddy Bears!

IV

THE NURSERY

IT WAS late that summer when The Princess Elizabeth went to live with her father and mother at 145, Piccadilly. She lived there for almost ten years, taking for her very own a beautiful, sunny nursery, arranged for her by her mother.

There was much that any little girl would like about this quiet old house in London. For The Princess Elizabeth it was a lovely home. At the back of the house there was a beautiful garden surrounded with tall shrubs and trees, an ideal place for little legs to romp and explore. From her nursery window one could see the roof-top of Grandma's house, for Buckingham Palace looked down upon the trees that stood between Elizabeth's window and the house where Grandfather lived.

When Elizabeth's straight, tiny legs grew long enough so that she could see out of the day-nursery window down onto busy Piccadilly, that window was her first view of the world of grown-ups. And what a busy world it was to be sure! What a wondrous game for wet and dreary London days when the garden was forbidden!

Soldiers! Sailors! Hurrying people! And hundreds and hundreds of crawling motor cars and big busses that the tall policeman could stop and start by the mere wave of his hand! If one listened carefully, the music of a Guards' Band from the palace or perhaps the tramp of marching feet would come in through that window-to-the-outside world, to fill two small ears with wonder and start a little tongue on a thousand and one questions.

Mother had made the second floor at 145, Piccadilly into a beautiful world for this child Princess to grow up in, and, as far as this story is concerned, it was her home. So I shall tell you more about it.

This nursery of large and wondrous windows was really an apartment of three rooms. The first was the day nursery with its window-to-the-outside world, for it was here that little "Lisabet" as she called herself, really lived and played. It was a very large room, yet not too large for so busy a tiny person as Lisabet. The walls were of a bright, golden colour that made it look as if the sun were always shining; and the carpet was coloured like ripe cherries ready to pick. There was a fireplace, of course, for how else could Santa Claus come down the chimney to visit the Princess? Two pictures of Mummy and Daddy, the Duke and Duchess of York, hung on the walls, and also a lovely painting of a little girl that Grandma, the Queen, had given her for her own sitting room.

In this room was Lisabet's chair, and no one dared to sit there without the permission of its owner. It was a wonderful chair, with leaping mountain goats jumping in play across the back. But the most wonderful thing about it was that if you sat upon a certain spot, it would play a gay, tinkling tune!

Then on another wall stood a tall mahogany cabinet, with glass doors on top, through which the funniest collection of little people and animals peered out at one. Near the cupboard were three hassocks that stood beneath the shade of two comfortable chesterfield chairs, where her grown-up visitors would sit to be shown the special toys and books.

All around the wall of the nursery were panel paintings of characters from fairy stories. Goldilocks and the Three Bears, Mother Goose, and The Fairy Princess. But best of all Lisabet liked Goldilocks and the Three Bears. It was this story that she first learned by heart.

When Mother would come to the nursery to tell her a bedtime story, for Lisabet loved bedtime stories, the little Princess would tell the Duchess all about the adventures of Goldilocks. And when both Mother and Father came to see her off to bed, Father had to be the "Big Bear," Mother the next "Biggest Bear," and Lisabet both the "Little Bear" and "Goldilocks" all at the same time.

Once Lisabet had been naughty, for even princesses can be naughty, you know, and her mother, to punish her, refused to tell the usual bedtime story.

"All right, Mummy! Lisabet will tell you a story," said the child after she had pleaded with her mother for some time for a story.

"Once upon a time," started Lisabet, sitting on a hassock, with her knees gathered in her arms, "there was a little fairy Princess called Lisabet, and she asked her Mummy for a story, and her Mummy wouldn't tell her a story, and so she ran away into the woods and a great big bear came along an' said 'Who's been eating my porridge?' An' he gobbled up Lisabet, and Lisabet's mummy dear never did see Lisabet any more, an' Lisabet's mummy dear wished she had told Lisabet a story so she wouldn't have been all gobbled up by the Big Bear!"

And her mummy dear, whom you now know as the Queen of England, admitted to her friends that Lisabet *did* get her story that night after all!

Peter was her favourite toy, when she was a tiny, tiny girl. Peter was just as small! In fact, Peter was a tupenny ha'penny little white rabbit not more than two inches long. But each and every night when the golden curls went to their pillow, Peter was always beside her in the white cot. In the daytime Peter went with her in the pocket of her overalls or in her rompers.

Peter was useful, too. You see, Lisabet did not like spinach and whenever spinach was offered her, she would put half of it on a special plate for Peter.

"Peter like spinach," Lisabet told her nurse. So the nurse next time gave the little Princess more spinach in order that both Peter and Lisabet might get what was good for them.

"Peter doesn't like spinach any more," admitted The Princess Elizabeth after that.

Elizabeth really loved Peter Rabbit. There was a day when Uncle George, the Duke of Kent, brought to the nursery a new toy which he hoped would capture the heart of his little niece. The young Duke demonstrated the toy in person. It was a fluffy dog that barked so loudly when you pressed his ears that it made the other toys in the cabinet almost jump up and down with surprise. Apparently the little Princess was delighted with her uncle's present.

A few days later, the Duke of Kent again visited The Princess Elizabeth, and, very much to his surprise,

the barking dog was not to be found anywhere.
At last he asked Lisabet what had happened to it.
The tiny Princess led Uncle George by the hand to
a dark cupboard just outside the nursery. There,
all by himself, was the mechanical dog.

"You see, Uncle George, he frightened poor little
Peter with his bowwows," she explained.

Besides Peter there were other favourites—a drake
that quacked most realistically and proudly sported
a green feather in his tail, and a silky-coated yellow-
brown dog. Always it was a toy animal, for although
she liked dolls, they never quite captured the fancy
of little Lisabet as much as the animals in her "zoo."

But we cannot leave the nursery without a peek
at Lisabet's first Doll House, the present of her
grandmother, Queen Mary. It was indeed a wonderful Doll House and her uncles, the Royal Princes,
were always bringing new bits of furniture for it,
until the sides almost puffed out like a pouter pigeon.

Her favourite uncle the Prince of Wales, when he
returned from Africa, even brought with him a tiny
set of native swords and spears made for him by a
native warrior. They were just the right size to
hang on the wall in the front hall of Lisabet's Doll
House.

"Mr. and Mrs. Milton live there," the imaginative
child would explain to her visitors. "And they

have a little girl named 'Lisabet.' " For hours on
end The Princess Elizabeth, acting the part of Mrs.
Milton, would play with the Doll House, send the
imaginary Lisabet to bed for being naughty, and
generally supervise the house.

But we must not forget to visit the other two
rooms of the second-floor nursery. The second
room is the night nursery and faces out on the
garden where there is no buzz of London traffic to
keep a tired little girl awake at night. It, too, has
a cosy fireplace before which tiny toes in sleepers
could curl with comfort on a cold winter's night.
In one corner is the baby's cot, to which the little
Princess objected for months, but which Mother
thought safest for her. In the opposite corner is
a washstand, bearing her wash-basin and china jug,
which is visited many times by a little girl with
grubby hands, particularly after playing in the
garden. A dressing table and a chest of drawers
with a comfortable chair for Mother or Nanny
complete the furniture of the room where a sleepy
Princess, sometimes unwillingly, sails off to the land
of dreams.

The third room of the nursery suite is the kitchen
where all of the baby Princess's meals are prepared.
It is here Lisabet first learned to cook. For the
Princess, you see, amongst other things, is an excel-

H.R.H. The Princess Elizabeth and H.R.H. Princess Margaret
Rose

lent little cook. Indeed, when she was but three
years' old, she made her own strawberry jam and
stored it, all correctly labelled, in rows of shining jars.
This, then, was the delightful home that Elizabeth
lived in and played in for nine happy years.

V

THE HUNT

NASEBY HALL is an ancient country house in beautiful Northamptonshire, the place where Cromwell so many hundreds of years ago defeated the King's Army in a fierce and mighty battle.

When her mother told her that they were going to Naseby Hall for the winter, Lisabet, who was not quite three, clapped her hands with joy. Not because of Oliver Cromwell and his Roundheads, as his soldiers were called, nor yet because of Naseby Hall itself—for all that it was a beautiful house for any little girl to live in—but rather because her mother explained that Father was going there to hunt. Lisabet jumped up and down with delight, for that would mean horses and hounds and a real live huntsman and red coats, and the open country. So it was at Naseby Hall, in what her father called "good hunting country," that Lisabet really fell in love with beautiful horses. In fact, Nurse had to watch the little Princess very closely, for she would

be running off to the stables at the slightest chance
at any time of the day.

Each morning she would fill her pockets with
sugar and toddle off to the stables, where big hunters
looked for a tiny girl that rubbed the velvet of their
noses and came with pockets full of sweets. And
what excitement there was when she was taken to
the kennels to see the hounds! They wagged their
tails for all the world like the metronome that tick-
tocked on the piano during music lessons!

Then there was the glorious day when Father said
she might see the hunt start off.

There is nothing that will send tingles up and
down anyone's backbone quicker than a fox hunt.
So Elizabeth found out this frosty morning.

First, of course, there are the hounds, ten couples
of them sniffing along the ground as if they had lost
something. They all keep close to the huntsman's
horse, for he is in charge of the hounds and knows
them all by name. With the huntsman are two
other red-coated riders known as whips, short for
whippers-in, and they help the huntsman take care
of the pack. These three riders are known as hunt
servants. I suppose they would be called in any
other sport, professionals.

On this particular morning, over fifty ladies and
gentlemen rode to the hunt, the gentlemen in coats

of red (that is called hunting pink). Some of the ladies rode astride and some rode side-saddle. The buttons and collars of the ladies' riding habits bore the name and colour of that particular hunt. The gentleman in charge of the hunt, and he always rides right behind the hounds and in front of all the other ladies and gentlemen, is the Master of Fox Hounds. He is called for short, the Master. He must be a hard and fearless rider, and he was.

It was not long before the huntsman had taken his hounds to a spot where the scent of a fox was picked up. The hounds started off.

"Ta-ra-aa."

The huntsman blew a blast on his horn, and off went the hunt across country! Over fields and ditches, walls and fences, Elizabeth could see the field of ladies and gentlemen spreading out, the harder riders not losing ground at all as the hounds raced at top speed after the fox. Then, from a convenient hilltop, she could see riderless horses tossing their bridle reins. For in every hunt there are falls at bad fences, and very often, aside from the fact that their gay coats are drenched and their silk hats battered, the hunters are injured. The little Princess could not watch the hunt for long because the fox ran straight away across country for more than twenty miles before he was run to earth. But what

Elizabeth did see made her long for the day when she, too, might be allowed to wear a hunt uniform and join in the chase.

These were happy days, but even so, they must end. For two or three days Elizabeth had noticed that Father and Mother talked quietly and looked worried. Even Nurse seemed quiet and forgetful of the happiness of so lovely a place. At last they told the little Princess that Grandfather was ill, and that everyone must go back to London at once.

Poor little Elizabeth! It was bad enough to have to leave Naseby, with its big hunters, its sweet-smelling stables, and the crunching of teeth as the hunters nibbled the hay. But it was much worse to know that Grandpa, the King, was sick. And so they all packed off to London again for the winter.

Each night when she said her prayers, Lisabet asked God to make Grandpa better, and millions of little English girls prayed with her. But of course, they did not finish their prayers as the little Princess did. "Please God, do make Grandpa better, so that he can play with Lisabet again."

God did make the King better, and four hundred million subjects the world over thanked Him, but none more fervently than his small granddaughter, The Princess Elizabeth.

On Christmas Eve Lisabet was allowed to stay up to hear the carol singers. But it didn't seem quite like Christmas to Lisabet. Whoever heard of Christmas away from Sandringham and Grandpa?

She heard them singing the beautiful old carol, "While Shepherds Watched Their Flocks by Night." "Glad tidings of great joy I bring to you and all mankind!" they sang. Little Lisabet lifted her chin from her hand. Her eyes widened. "I know Old Man Kind, Mummy!" she shrieked excitedly. "Old Man Kind is dear Grandpa! He's very old and he's very, very kind."

The Princess Elizabeth was not wrong, for very soon glad tidings did come of her dear grandfather. They came the day after Christmas at one of her special tea parties given her by the Queen at Buckingham Palace. Grandmother had let her bring Lady Mary Cambridge, her friend who is just a little older than Lisabet. That afternoon at the Palace, Grandma promised Lisabet that she could soon go and look after Grandpa herself, and tell her Grandpa how, during his long illness, she had each day brought sugar for the King's parrot, to cheer him up. For the poor parrot was quite miserable when his kind master was away.

So it was that the Princess went to look after her grandfather at Craigwell House by the seaside, where the King was slowly getting strong and well again. Each day Lisabet would run beside the King's wheel chair or sit and tell him stories that she knew would make him better quickly. She told him of the horses and the hounds; and how Father Christmas had come down the chimney and left the good little girl at 145, Piccadilly such wonderful things, rocking horses and dolls and lions and tigers.

Grandfather laughed and grew strong. He told Lisabet wonderful stories of the sea and all sorts of strange places away over the ocean, and of ships and the great men who sailed them. For you see, Grandfather was not only a King, he was a very great and brave sailor who loved the sea.

"I made Grandpa all well, Mummy," the Princess later told the Duchess, and the great doctors were not at all certain that she was not right.

It was a happy Princess who went back to Naseby Hall that spring with her mother and father. And it was there she spent her third birthday.

What a wonderful birthday party that was! Who do you think came to her party to share the cake with three bright red candles? Why, all the boys and girls from Naseby School, and such a time they had at the Princess's birthday party, with just enough cake to go around. And such wonderful

presents! A toy Shetland pony from Mother and
Father, and a real live dog, the perkiest little Cairn
terrier you could ever wish to see, from Uncle David,
the Prince of Wales, who had come rushing across
the world from dark Africa to help Lisabet make
Grandpa well.

VI

FIRST LESSONS

BEING a Princess, even a tiny one of less than four years, is not all toys and tea parties, for there is so much to learn—things that ordinary little girls do not have to bother their heads about for years and years.

Lisabet made up her mind to learn the alphabet so that she could say it off by heart on her fourth birthday. And she did. Not only did the little Princess say the alphabet, but she sang it. She likes to sing, and that is how she learned the alphabet. Every night before it came time for her mother to tell her a bedtime story, she would sing her "A B C" song with her mother.

Then there was this counting business.

"One—two—three —— five," the tiny Princess would lisp. Then Mummy would start her over again and again, until at last that troublesome "four" was found and put in its right place. Then, every day, there was a singing lesson in the nursery with the Duchess, her mother. Lisabet liked her singing lessons, "best of all my learnings," she told a little friend one day in the garden. And she does sing nicely.

Indeed, the tiny Princess had learned a great deal before the time came for her to blow out four candles on a birthday cake. Not only did her mother teach her, but there was Grandma, Queen Mary, patiently to instruct and advise her.

Grandma it was who gave her the most wonderful set of building blocks, all made of different kinds of wood. There were ebony from the jungles, maple from Canada, and oak from England. As she played with them, Elizabeth learned of fifty different kinds of wood and of the lands in Grandpa's Empire where they came from. It was not only from the building blocks that Elizabeth learned her early geography, for Uncle David would come and sit with her by the hour and tell her of the far-off places he had visited. Lisabet liked that. She would sit with her arms about her knees, her big, blue eyes wide open, and listen to Uncle David till the gooseberries dropped off the bushes in the garden. History she learned, too, while other little girls had not yet started to toddle off to kindergarten. The Queen decided that the best way for any little girl to learn history was to visit the places where history was made. And so Elizabeth not only saw the Tower of London and the Houses of Parliament in picture books, but she also drove to them with her mother or her grandmother the Queen, and heard the wonderful stories of yesterday told to her while her two small white shoes stood firmly on the self-same spot.

Elizabeth loved dancing, especially the Scottish reels taught her by her mother and her nurse. In fact, she delighted her Royal grandparents by being able to do a Highland reel for them on her fourth Christmas.

But one of the most difficult things for a healthy little lady of less than four is to master court manners, and to appear always with a Princess-like bearing. In her fourth year Lisabet was told that she must always curtsey to Grandfather and Grandmother, for they are "the King and Queen." Now, the Princess loved her grandfather and grandmother very dearly, and she could not think of any better way to greet them than by running to them and giving each a special big kiss. So she became a little rebel, and it was only after a great deal of explaining that she was made to realize just why she must curtsey first. Particularly, she should do this when there were grown-ups present.

The very next day the King called in to see his little granddaughter. As soon as he came into the nursery, Princess Elizabeth swept a low curtsey to His Majesty—but, unfortunately, *with her back to the King.*

"There you are, Grandpa," she laughed. "You see, I did curtsey!" And the good King made the nursery ring with his strong sailor's laugh as he gathered Lisabet up in his arms.

Court manners and courtesy were learned by the Princess, most of them from her queenly grandmother, from the time when she first walked. You see, Lisabet saw more of her grandparents than most little girls do. Nearly always once a week, and very often twice, she visited Buckingham Palace or stayed at Windsor Castle or Sandringham, the other two homes of the King and Queen.

Tea with Queen Mary has always been a great delight to both Lisabet and her grandmother. Indeed, from the time when the Princess was less than two years, down to the present day, they have been the brightest moments of her busy days. A special little stool, with a low table beside it, was provided by the Queen for Lisabet. There the Princess would sit and chatter away throughout the tea hour to her grandmother. Another small chair always stood between the Princess and her grandmother. This was for the favourite doll whom the Princess helped to tea, served in a tiny gold

and rose teacup. There was always one rule
to be obeyed, and that was that Lisabet should
not have more than one cake! Mummy had seen
to that!

Very often the Queen would take Elizabeth
driving, and the people soon noticed that their tiny
Princess was bowing and smiling to them as she
passed, just as the Queen did. Slowly but surely
Elizabeth was learning the gracious manners that
must be part of the training, not only of a Princess,
but of all little ladies.

One of the little Princess's fondest possessions was
a tricycle which she used to ride often in the park
when she went there with her nurse. One day her
two small cousins, Gerald and George Lascelles,
were playing with her in the garden and all three
wanted to ride the new tricycle at once.

"I think it should be ladies first," spoke up
Elizabeth.

"No, it shouldn't. It should be visitors first,"
said Master Gerald, grasping the handlebars.

"No, no, no!" shrieked Lisabet. "I am a
Princess and it should be Princesses first!"

For that her two boy cousins had no arguments,
and Elizabeth mounted her beloved tricycle. Then
the little Princess began to realize that she had not
acted in the manner of a lady or a Princess.

"Oh, well, you have first go, anyway," she said getting off and handing over the tricycle to her cousins.

But Elizabeth did not always so easily realize her mistakes and had to be punished just as any other child who has been naughty.

Once when she was shopping in a great London store with her grandmother she kept begging Queen Mary to leave.

"Why, Elizabeth, I thought you liked shopping?" said her grandmother.

"I know, Grandma, I do like shopping. But there are such a lot of people standing outside waiting to see me when I come out the front door!"

Elizabeth was taken home in disgrace that day. Her grandmother had the motor car taken around to the back entrance of the store where no people could see a little girl who had that day not acted as a Princess should.

Another day when The Princess Elizabeth was playing in the gardens at Buckingham Palace, she ran off the lawns, across a gravel path, and past a six-foot Guardsman sentry.

"Crash." The Guardsman slapped the butt of his rifle. "Slap." His left hand hit the sling till the white buff flew off it, and he made it ring like a rifle shot against the walls. "Crash." The rifle snapped down in front of the sentry and one boot heel came back behind the other all at once.

He had presented arms, the highest salute a sentry can give, and one always given by soldiers on duty to generals and members of the Royal Family.

The bayonet steel flashed in the sunlight as the sentry presented arms to the Princess. At first it frightened Lisabet. Then she giggled and ran back again. Again the Guardsman presented arms. Lisabet tried it again and again. This was a good game, and such fun! But not so for the unhappy soldier whose neck by this time was as scarlet as his tunic. An officer seeing what was happening brought The Princess Elizabeth's game to an end by telling her nurse. Then poor Lisabet was again in trouble.

But The Princess Elizabeth's naughtiest act was throwing a teaspoon at her grandfather, who was teasing her during tea at Buckingham Palace. Lisabet was broken-hearted over that, for she loved her grandfather dearly. But there are times when the best and most loving little girls are naughty. However, that did not make the Princess, who cried herself to sleep that night, feel the least bit better at being rude to her grandfather.

Lisabet, happy child, could never quite understand why people should not treat her as an ordinary person.   Often, particularly during the tourist season, when she was playing in the garden, people would stare at her through the iron railings, or poke cameras through the shrubs.

But Elizabeth is a friendly child.   One day, when she was playing in the garden with her playmate, Lady Mary Elizabeth Stewart, who lived next door, she led her friend by the hand to a group of people who were watching her play.

"This is Mary," she said.   She smiled at the peekers from the depth of her warm little heart. And she wondered why the people, after bowing, scuttled off, for all the world like so many rabbits surprised in the woods.

"They must be afraid of us," she said wistfully to Lady Mary, and the two went back to their dolls and carriages.

Indeed, this golden-haired Princess with the beautiful blue eyes often surprised people.   One of the *most* surprised was a great lady who had called to see her mother, the Duchess.   While sitting waiting in the drawing room she was shocked to see a tiny figure in a dust cap come into the room and vigorously commence polishing the furniture.

"Good afternoon," said the little house-cleaner, who was also armed with a toy carpet sweeper. "Isn't it terrible how the dust collects?"   And with a final polish of the table top, she swept, hard at work, through another door, with the carpet sweeper working in a most business-like fashion.

The lady caller still finds it hard to realize that the little person with the duster and the carpet sweeper will probably one day be her Queen!

VII

A PART OF CANADA

WINDSOR PARK offers many wonderful things for a little Princess to enjoy, and it was a delighted Elizabeth who made a wonderful discovery tucked away in the Park, in the shadow of the castle. What do you think it was? A Canadian bungalow, built by Canadian woodsmen as a gift to her grandfather when the Canadian Forestry Corps were felling giant trees in Windsor Park during the war.

To be quite exact, it wasn't Lisabet that really discovered the Canadian bungalow, although she liked to think she did. One bright afternoon, her Grandfather, the King, took her to see it as he had done nearly all his guests at Windsor since the war. The King explained to Elizabeth that the long porch in front was called a verandah, for, you see, there are not many verandahs in England, and the Princess had never seen one before. She was delighted with the log cabin with its four big windows looking out on the verandah and the charming rustic fence that ran all round it. The fence seemed to say, "Inside me is a part of Canada."

One afternoon, Elizabeth was out walking with her grandfather and grandmother, the King and Queen.

"Will you come to Lisabet's own house for tea now, Grandma and Grandpa?" she asked.

"Why, certainly, my dear," replied the Queen. "But where is your own house?"

"It's in Canada, Grandma. Grandpa knows where it is." And Elizabeth ran off as fast as her legs would carry her, into the Canadian log bungalow behind the rustic fence which made it part of Canada.

Soon the King and Queen were on the verandah, and The Princess Elizabeth met them with a pretty curtsey.

"Will you come in to tea, your Majesty?" she asked her grandfather.

"Certainly, my dear," he replied, with twinkling eyes. "But what are you going to do for dish——?" but here the Queen silenced the King.

But The Princess Elizabeth *did* have an imagination, and even though there was no tea, or for that matter, no tea service, she did pour tea and help her grandfather and grandmother to cream and sugar and the most luscious cakes.

"I have enjoyed your tea party so much," the Queen said, after her tenth cup. The King, her grandfather, said so too.

"And I think your bungalow is charming, my child," he remarked. "In fact, if you will pardon me, Miss Canada, I would say it is *some* house," he added with that quick twinkle in his kind eyes that belongs to all great sailors.

Little Elizabeth went to Windsor Castle for her fourth birthday party and what a wonderful birthday it was for the Princess! No fairy Princess out of any picture book could have had a birthday in a more wondrous place than Windsor Castle. Her birthday came during Easter week, with "Easter Eggs and Easter Bunnies making thicker icing on the birthday cake," as one little boy said. Furthermore, her birthday was on Bank Holiday, so all England could come to her party.

Windsor Castle is the traditional home of English Kings, and has been so for hundreds and hundreds of years. It isn't very far from London, only a little more than twenty miles. But you would never think you were so close to the largest city in the world, for the castle is set in the midst of a "huge" Park, called "Windsor Great Park." It *is* indeed a great park, over twenty miles square, and covers about thirteen thousand acres of the most wonderful woods and park lands.

William the Conqueror, who was King of England eight hundred seventy years ago, was the first to make Windsor Castle his home. The sound of his hunting horn used to ring through the trees, and his arrows fell into the very green sod that Elizabeth's feet now walked upon. Since that time all the Kings of England have walked and ridden through this beautiful woodland park.

You may be sure that the little Princess was up bright and early with the sun, on this her fourth birthday, which was a glorious holiday for all the people in the land.

Her two little cousins, Lord Lascelles and the Honourable Gerald Lascelles, sons of her aunt, the Princess Royal, had come with their mother to Windsor, to attend Elizabeth's birthday party. And the two boys hurried Elizabeth out (if she needed hurrying, which I doubt very much), to see the Changing of the Guard, early in the morning.

There are four great regiments whose honoured duty it is to guard the King's palaces. These are the Grenadier Guards, the Coldstream Guards, the Scots Guards, and the Irish Guards. And what splendid soldiers these Guardsmen are! All over six feet tall, and in their high bearskins they looked like huge giants to the Princess.

Elizabeth loved soldiers. In fact, one day when someone asked her what she liked best of all, she said, "Dogs, horses, and soldiers." So you see the

Princess did not need much encouragement to go out that morning to see the Changing of the Guard, which is a very splendid ceremonial drill of which the Guards are very proud.

Standing alone just in front of her two cousins, Elizabeth watched the whole ceremony very gravely. Then she caught sight of the Pipers of the Regiment, and—I'll let you into a secret if you will promise not to tell the Coldstreams, the Grenadiers, or the Irish Guardsmen—The Princess Elizabeth likes the Scots Guards best of all because they have Pipers, and the skirl of the pipes always makes delicious little tunes go running up and down her back. So off went Elizabeth to inspect the Pipers of this great regiment whose historic predecessors fought in fifty mighty battles long before the Great War. Then she marched back to her position on the Great Square within the castle.

The Old Guard, as the company who were being relieved are called, were then marched off, and The Princess Elizabeth, her back as straight as any Guardsman's, returned the salute of the officer who was in command.

"The little Princess should have been a Prince," said this officer in the mess, afterwards. "Four years old today, and you would think she was a graduate of Sandhurst!" That was a splendid compliment, for you see, Sandhurst is the military school from which British officers graduate.

Elizabeth was not the only person to see the Changing of the Guard that morning, for as I said before, it was a holiday and hundreds of people had gathered at the castle gates to witness the ceremony. The little Princess was quite sure they had all come to her birthday party, so off she went toward the gates to blow them kisses, to wave her hand, and to thank them all for coming.

When Elizabeth closed her eyes in her cot on the night of her birthday, she was thinking of a new friend who had come to her that day. It was the finest Shetland pony that you ever laid eyes on, for that was Grandpa's gift to his small Princess. And she was thinking also of a wonderful toy motor car that could be pedalled ever so fast and had a real horn. This had been given her by her Uncle George, Duke of Kent.

Which should she ride first in the morning? Then the next thing she knew it was morning, and the sun was streaming in through the nursery window.

The first royal personage whom the sentry on duty saw coming out of the Castle gate that morning was the Princess, her tiny legs almost lost to sight in the shaggy coat of her Shetland pony, Peggy. The sentry presented arms with a crash! Peggy jumped forward suddenly, but game little Elizabeth remembered to do two things: to stick on the saddle and to shout a hurried, "Good morning" in reply to the Guardsman's salute. It was Elizabeth's first adventure on horseback, but she was to have many, many more.

Almost as exciting was the morning in the same month when she was pedalling her toy motor car as fast as she could around a corner and ran bang into the legs of a big, fat policeman!

"That," said Uncle David, Prince of Wales, with mock severity, "is reckless driving, and I also suspect you are driving without a license."

So Uncle David, who is always lots of fun, made her a special license and gave her the nicest little leather folder to carry it in. And every time a policeman should see her driving recklessly he was to take her license and write down the charge therein.

Altogether it was a most wonderful birthday month at Windsor.

VIII

A LITTLE SISTER

LATE that summer as usual, Lisabet went to visit her other grandfather and grandmother, at their castle in the Highlands of Scotland.

The Princess Elizabeth had been there many, many times, but this visit she would never forget. For one thing, Elizabeth was older, and her busy tongue was ever ready with a thousand questions that tumbled over themselves to be answered by grown-ups. There were so many wonderful things to ask about Glamis Castle where the Scottish nobleman and his good wife, Lady Strathmore, lived.

The castle is one of the oldest in Scotland, and is filled to the top of its many grey turrets with rich history. It was from this castle that Bonnie Prince Charlie had fled, leaving behind him under his pillow a watch that was shown to The Princess Elizabeth. Of those far-off days, when the Royal Stuarts ruled and when brave men went forth with their clans to war, caring little whether theirs was a forlorn hope or not, this castle speaks from every stone.

Little Elizabeth of York learned there of the pride that is the true Highlander's. She was shown yards and yards of very beautiful tapestry which now hangs on the walls of her Scottish grandfather's billiard room. On this tapestry were pictures worked in threads by the women of Strathmore in the days when Knights wore great heavy suits of armour to go forth to battle. Lisabet played hide-and-seek on the great stairs of stone, up which wounded King Malcolm had been carried by his men-at-arms. The little Princess saw in the castle hall a large buff coat, and she was told that this very coat had been worn by John Graham of Claver-house. And on another wall her wondering little blue eyes saw this great warrior's mighty claymore (a large, two-edged sword).

The rooms of the castle have such queer names that a little girl is bound to ask questions about them. "Duncan's Rooms," "The old Armoury," "Hangman's Room," "Prince Charlie's Room," "King Malcolm's Room." It was here that Eliza-beth learned to tell to what clan the wearer of a certain tartan belonged, and heard the valiant history of the Scottish clans themselves.

To a little girl, even to a real Princess, Glamis was a fairy castle, in a fairyland of yesterday. Even the town of Glamis with its one main street seemed to fit into the picture completely, for every fairyland castle must have a town for its turrets to look down upon.

But even this fairyland world was not the reason why The Princess Elizabeth will always remember this particular visit to the Highlands. Strangely enough, she was the very last person in the castle to hear of the surprise which she can never forget.

One night there was great excitement in the old castle. But Elizabeth did not know of this, for she was sleeping in the moonlight that swept onto her nursery cot through the old leaded diamond panes of the castle windows. Yes, there was a great deal of excitement—telephones buzzing, motor cars arriving and leaving, telegrams coming in baskets full. Soon, it seemed as if the whole of Scotland was agog with excitement, and no free Highlander went to bed that night till the cock crowed. People ran helter-skelter into the streets laughing and cheering, while press cars raced for the nearest telegraph office. Soon the news was cabled to the four ends of the earth, and Scots the world over waxed proud and boastful.

Still Elizabeth slept on in her nursery cot, as all good children must do. People, millions of people in every country in the world, smiled as they read their morning papers, and said, "How nice for little Princess Elizabeth!"

But Elizabeth was eating her porridge and drinking her milk, not knowing of the surprise to come. Then nurse told her the glad tidings.

"You have a lovely baby sister," said Nannie.

"But I haven't a sister," exclaimed Elizabeth.

"Oh, but you have! The dearest little sister came to the Castle last night while you were sleeping."

For several minutes Elizabeth tried to realize what her nurse had told her, then she jumped up and down with delight. A real baby sister of her very own! How lovely! A little sister to play with, to share Peggy, and to take for rides in her toy motor car! The Princess Elizabeth felt that life was now complete.

"A baby sister to look after," she said. "Can I see her now, Nannie?"

Elizabeth was taken to see her new sister. Such a wee thing she was, wrapped in yards and yards of white shawls.

"Isn't she pretty, Mummy. What are we going to call her?"

"Margaret Rose. Isn't that a nice name, Elizabeth?"

"Yes, Mummy. But she's so, *so* tiny, I think I shall call her Bud."

"Why 'Bud,' Elizabeth?"

"Well, she isn't really a rose yet, is she, Mummy dear? She is really only a bud."

Father kissed and hugged Lisabet when she said that, and Mummy too. But she was Lisabet no more. Now that she had a baby sister to take care of she was Elizabeth. And she did look after Margaret Rose always, as you shall learn.

That night Elizabeth saw a red glow light up the the sky on a distant hill, as a huge bonfire crackled and spluttered. The fire had been lit by four Scottish girls with as many torches, for the good people of Glamis had their own way of telling the world that this day a princess had been born to Scotland

IX

THE FIRST WEDDING

THERE were several reasons why The Princess Elizabeth at five began to feel that she was quite a grown-up little person, and it is quite fair to say that her dear baby sister was not the least of these.

Elizabeth was just five years and six months old to the day when she took a grown-up's part in the outside-the-nursery-window world, and wore her first long blue gown. Surely that would make any small lady feel very much grown up! It did The Princess Elizabeth, so I shall tell you about it.

It so happened that Lady May Cambridge, daughter of Major-General the Earl of Athlone (brother of Queen Mary) and of Princess Alice, the Countess of Athlone, fell very much in love with a tall and handsome officer, Captain Henry Abel Smith and in due course, this fine-looking Captain of the Horse Guards won the hand of the charming young lady who was niece of the Queen.

The King announced that his niece would marry this gallant soldier in October of that year (1931). At once

the people surmised that the wedding would be a
magnificent and lavish one, possibly to be held in
the King's Chapel at Windsor Castle, of which the
Earl of Athlone was governor. The newspapers
made much of the betrothal for, you see, although
he was an Officer of His Majesty's Horse Guards,
and a descendant of one of Cromwell's most trusted
lieutenants, Captain Abel Smith was, after all, a
commoner. That means he was not of Royal blood.
Yet he was taking in marriage the only daughter of
a Prince and a Princess. But to be sure, The Princess
Elizabeth did not worry her head about that, for she
had seen for herself what a fine gentleman the
officer was, and secretly admired the way he wore
the brilliant helmet and blue full dress of the Horse
Guards.

It was a grand wedding, but when the newspapers
talked of Windsor Chapel, they surmised, as newspapers very often do, entirely wrong. When the
announcement was made that the wedding of the
year would be held in the quaint church of a Sussex
village, how that little village of Balcome did gasp
when it heard the news! The gossip buzzed so much
around the hedges and walls that you would have
thought millions and millions of honey bees had
been let loose on fair Sussex. It was not that Balcome
lacked the right to see their Lady May married.

Indeed, it had every right, for her father's estate was near by, and she had grown up in the midst of the villagers.   But then, people had talked so much about a grand wedding in the King's castle, up London way, that they felt they had been forgotten. They could hardly believe their ears when the news came!   And how the choir boys of Balcome Church almost sang their lungs away over the hedge tops, preparing themselves for the great event!

Imagine Elizabeth's delight when her mother told her that she would take the part of a bridesmaid at this delightful wedding.   With her would be three charming young ladies—Lady Mary Cambridge, her little friend, Miss Rosemary Fraser, and Miss Jennifer Bevan, all just a bit older than Elizabeth.   Then there were to be eight grown-up bridesmaids, too— as if they really counted!   They included Princess Ingrid of Sweden and Princess Sibylla of Saxe-Coburg and Gotha, which meant after all that some attention would have to be paid these important ladies.

At last came the day of the wedding.   It was a bright, sunny day, but The Princess Elizabeth was so thrilled and excited that she hardly noticed the sun at all.

She and the three other small bridesmaids were all dressed in blue.   And let me tell you, there was not a good cottager of Balcome, nor yet a prince of

The night nursery, and the day nursery, where the Princesses
entertain their friends

the Blood Royal that did not think The Princess
Elizabeth was the sweetest little girl in all England
that day.

Her frock was of a powder blue that matched her
beautiful eyes. It was Victorian in style, with a
high bodice and a skirt that swept the ground about
her tiny silver slippers. On her head she wore a
Juliet cap of plaited blue ribbon to match her frock,
and in her hands she carried a fragrant posy of many
dainty flowers.

Though she may some day be Queen-Empress of
this mighty Empire, Elizabeth will never forget the
thrill of leading the wedding party. Along the path
and up the bank under the shade of the yew trees,
and down the main aisle of that quaint old church
of St. Mary they walked. Certainly the thousands
who gathered from near and far to see the wedding
said they had never beheld so pretty a sight.

The little Princess did not falter once, nor did she
look back. She remembered afterwards that, while
listening to Archbishop Carter of South Africa read
the Service, she had wished that Captain Henry Abel
Smith had worn his full-dress Horse Guard's uniform.
She thought it much more striking than a morning
coat and striped trousers. And how pretty the bride
looked in her ivory satin, and veil of rare old lace.
It was the same veil that Elizabeth's grandmother

5

had worn when she had wed the King, who was then Prince George.

Once, and only once, did Elizabeth feel the slightest bit nervous. Then she caught sight of her grandmother, Queen Mary, looking very calm and regal. And just then Uncle David caught Elizabeth's eye and smiled. How could any little girl be nervous under their eyes? The Princess decided that she was not.

After the wedding they all went to Brantbridge Park, where the Earl and Countess of Athlone lived, for the jolliest of parties. And how delighted she was when Grandma told her that she had done so well at the church that she was proud of her!

The Princess Elizabeth inspected the wonderful presents, over six hundred of them. Among them was the diamond chain and pendant that had been the gift of the King and Queen to the bride. The Princess thought she had never seen anything so wonderful as the giant wedding cake that weighed nearly a hundred pounds. It was a thrilling moment when Lady May took her husband's long cavalry sword and thrust it into the cake for the first cut.

Then there came the Court photographers to take official pictures of the wedding party! How very grown up and important a little girl could feel at times thought Elizabeth, and however would she remember it all to tell Margaret Rose?

A few years later, Captain Henry Abel Smith and Lady May had a daughter of their very own, and what do you think they called her? Why, Elizabeth! That made the Princess feel very proud, and what is more, it gave her the opportunity of telling Margaret Rose all over again about the wonderful wedding in Sussex when she was first allowed to be a real grown-up, with a lovely powder-blue gown that came right down to the toes of her silver slippers.

X

"Y BWYTHYN BACH"

"ENGLISH recitation, by The Princess Elizabeth."
"French recitation, *Au Clair de Lune*, by The
Princess Elizabeth."

Thus did the Princess write in her own round hand
the opening numbers of the charming programme she
herself arranged to entertain guests at her sixth
birthday party. You see, for a little girl of six, the
Princess was quite grown up in her ideas.

Of course, Grandfather and Grandmother did help
with her birthday party. For they permitted it to
be held in the great Oak Room of Windsor Castle,
and the King himself ordered his chef to bake the
cake and charged him to see that it was a fitting
birthday cake for the finest little lady in all the land.
All the Royal Family came to Elizabeth's party and
joined in the tea in the garden of the Castle. How
her three uncles did applaud when she had finished
her recitations and made a charming curtsey! But
those six sputtering candles that made Margaret
Rose clap her tiny hands with glee, spelt the end of

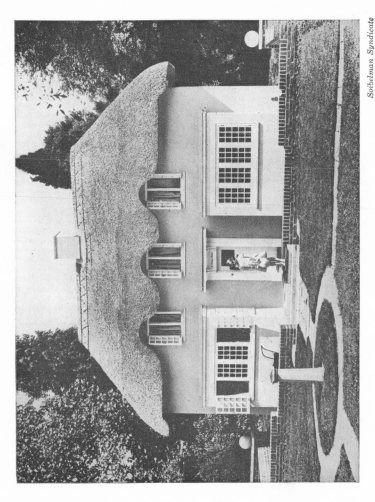

Soibelman Syndicate

A Royal hostess at home at "Y Bwythyn Bach"

carefree baby days for Elizabeth. For now she must devote the best part of each and every day to learn her lessons. Although she could, as she had so well proved that day, already recite both in French and English, still, there were years and years of books and lessons ahead of her.

Even now, as she laughed and played through her sixth birthday, decorators were plying hammer and brush to make her a schoolroom in the Royal Lodge at Windsor Park. The Lodge was the summer home of her father and mother, given to them by the King. Even the warm, lazy days of summer would not mean holidays for Elizabeth now. She had begged her mother to let her go to school with other children, and her mother would have liked nothing better than to allow her to do this. As the Princess had pointed out, her Royal uncles and her grandfather, the King, had all gone to school with other boys. But the people thought it wiser that Elizabeth should be taught her lessons at home. So Mother had arranged for the loveliest of ladies to teach her. Elizabeth did not mind. "I really like to learn things," she said, "and know about far-off places."

But we must not run away from Elizabeth's birthday party, for it brought Elizabeth a present that she still enjoys, and Margaret Rose with her.

It was indeed unfortunate, but it so happened that The Princess Elizabeth was not to see this wonderful present until some days after her birthday party, though that was not the wish of the good people who gave it to her. They really intended it as a surprise for her on her birthday.

It was all very mysterious. The Duke and Duchess had gone all the way to Cardiff, which is in Wales, before her birthday to look at this present and thank the good people who gave it. This, of course, they had not told the Princess, for as I said before, the present was to have been a surprise. But it didn't get to Windsor in time, because it took fire and half burnt up on the long road from Cardiff!

And what do you think the present was? When I tell you, I know you will understand why Elizabeth and Margaret Rose were so excited when they saw it that they forgot all about its being late.

It was the dearest and nicest play house you ever laid eyes upon! It had a thatched roof and real rooms to play in. It came from all the people in Wales! How Elizabeth wished she could write and thank each one of them!

Now, I know you will ask: However did the present catch fire? A search was made all over Wales for someone who could move the house holus-bolus (all at once), to Windsor, and set it down right in Elizabeth's garden. And at last a man with a giant truck was found. The truck was so big that it was driven by a steam engine. Off he started for London town with the little thatched house trundling along behind him on wheels. But, alas! One of the sparks from the steam engine flew on to the straw roof, and that is why the house from Wales did not get to Windsor Park by April twenty-first. I know you will feel sorry for the people of Wales who had their wonderful present burnt up, but so that you should not feel too badly about it, I will tell you that they had insured the house for four thousand dollars. And so, in no time, it was restored and on its way again to the Princess's garden.

"Why, it's just like two birthdays, Mummy!" said Princess Elizabeth, as she ran to see the house, her very own house, for the first time.

"An' my birfday, too, Mummy," broke in Margaret Rose, all excited.

I think the best way I can tell you of this wonderful house that Elizabeth and Margaret Rose still play in is to take you there on a visit.

In the first place, such a jewel of a tiny residence should have the right setting. For instance, to leave it out in a bare field where there were no trees would have been shameful. Therefore, the beautiful rose garden of the Lodge, with its wealth of flowers all the year around, and its cool, sheltering trees, was an ideal corner in which to tuck away this dream house.   That, of course, was the first thing to be noticed.

Elizabeth walked up to the front door along a new flagstone path that ran around a little sundial, which matched the house to a crossed "t." Then she stopped, all out of breath with excitement. And this is what she saw!

There were three cunning little windows upstairs that opened their sashes with tiny square panes towards the garden.   The thatched straw roof crowned with a square, squat chimney was cut away at the edges so that the upstairs windows could peek out.   On each side of the front door were two long casement windows, each in four sections.   The front door, which caused the Duke of York, who was a very tall daddy, to duck his head as he entered, was just the nicest front door Elizabeth had ever seen. Over it was inscribed in Welsh, the following:

"Y BWYTHYN BACH"

which means "The Little House."

Now, although you can be sure that The Princess Elizabeth did not stop then to measure it, I think I had better tell you the size of the Little House so that you will know what it looked like.   You see,

Elizabeth did not have to measure it for she could
see it. It is twenty-two feet wide, fifteen feet high,
and eight feet from the front to the back door as the
crow flies, (if crows ever did fly in a house, which I
very much doubt).

Elizabeth walked into the hallway, with its stair-
case leading upstairs and then ran into the living
room. This room was panelled in white, with an
oak floor. And, lo and behold, over the real fireplace
there hung a most beautiful picture of the Duchess
of York, the Princess's mother. All the furniture in
the living room was in old Welsh style with the
exception of the radio, which you can be sure was
one of the most modern.

Then into the kitchen went Elizabeth. Here was
a lovely casement window, running almost full
length, to let in plenty of sunlight. And what a
business-like little kitchen! A tiny gas stove with
an oven, all not two feet high, a sink with running
water, both hot and cold, and even an electric
refrigerator.

Elizabeth's legs could hardly get her upstairs fast
enough to see the bedroom and to look out of the
windows. Yes, and like the downstairs bedrooms,
it was completely furnished. There was an oak bed,
just four feet long and two feet wide, and beside the
bed a cot for her doll, Julie, and wardrobes to match

both. Then into the bathroom, and, would you believe it, there was even a tiny bath, just a little over three feet long, and a hand basin, exactly twenty-two inches wide! The most modern bathroom equipment, and all built to scale, to match The Little House!

What an exciting day that was, not only for The Princess Elizabeth but also for Princess Margaret Rose.

"This is my house, Mummy, and I want to look after it all myself."

"I do, too, Sis," piped up the tiniest Princess.

And, from then on, they did, for to this very day these two little girls look after The Little House. They dust and scrub it, wash and iron the gingham curtains, and polish the windows. Elizabeth even cooks on the little gas range that is no bigger than your family breadbox. And you should hear them scolding their dogs for not wiping their paws on the door mat!

XI

THE TROOPING OF THE COLOUR

YOU may rest assured that long before this time
the people of England loved The Princess Elizabeth very dearly. They loved her because she was
their Princess of York, it is true. But they loved her
more because she was such a good, kind little girl,
as her father and mother had wanted her to be ever
since the first day she came to stay at Bruton Street.

Now, of course, the people could not very well
see her at home, 145, Piccadilly, or at the Royal
Lodge in Windsor Great Park, or in her own little
Welsh house, any more than the majority of people
see you or me in our home or summer cottage.
But they did see a great deal of her at the public
functions which she attended with her father and
mother. And it was there that the people's fondest
hopes were realized, for her actions proved indeed
that she was a delightful personality, as well as a
Princess.

I think the biggest reason why the people of the
Empire came to love this Princess was the thoughtful

way she always looked after her sister, Princess Margaret Rose. You know it is very easy, when you are a big sister, to forget the smaller one sometimes. But not The Princess Elizabeth! She was always close to Margaret Rose, and her first thought was always for her little sister.

One day the two Princesses were taken to see a circus at the Olympia in London. Now there is nothing The Princess Elizabeth enjoys more than a circus, but this was the first circus the tiny Princess had seen, and so it was all new and strange to her little eyes.

The two were breathlessly watching performers on the flying trapeze, when a clown, wishing to delight the two Royal Princesses, came right up to the Royal box. His face was painted white and his lips were a bright scarlet. His sudden appearance did not amuse Margaret Rose. She had never seen a clown before and he frightened her. She shrank back into her seat, a very scared little girl. Now, any big sister who was enjoying the circus so much might have been excused had she exclaimed impatiently, "Don't be silly, he's only a clown!" But not The Princess Elizabeth. She stepped forward quickly, between her sister and the fearsome clown, and shook hands with the gentleman of the white face and red lips. Before he left, Princess Margaret

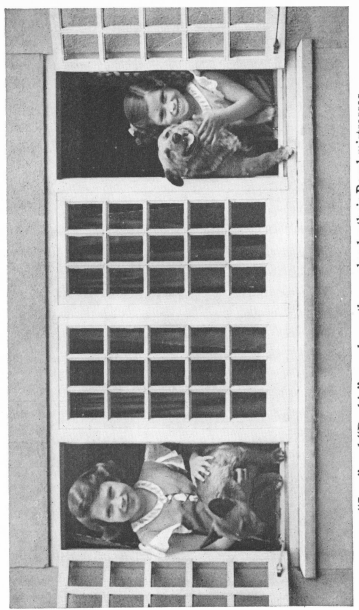

"Jane" and "Dookie" are shown the garden by their Royal mistresses

Rose had also shaken hands with him, her fright forgotten.

Of course the people know that acts such as this are an example of the daily life and lovely dispositions of these two Royal little sisters, just as the way you act towards your brother and sister when you are away from home, tells strangers of your disposition.

As a matter of fact, Margaret Rose seemed to have completely fitted into the happy nursery at 145, Piccadilly. In the Sheraton bookcase, Elizabeth's toys were told to move over and make room for the playthings of Margaret Rose. And instead of one little girl putting all her toys away when she had finished playing with them, two little girls now did so.

Instead of one small set of tea china, two appeared. Elizabeth's were blue and white, with a delightful pattern made up of two blackbirds and the motto "Two for Joy," and her sister's were pink and white, with a love bird perched on a sprig of Scottish heather.

The washstand in the night nursery, instead of bearing a single wash basin and water jug, now held two sets, one a bit larger than the other.

By now, The Princess Elizabeth had attended all the great ceremonies and functions that London is so proud of, and each time she returned home she would tell Margaret Rose all about them. However, it was not long before the two Royal sisters always went together to these great events.

It was a thrilling occasion when Elizabeth was first taken by her father and mother to see the Royal Military Tournament at the Olympia. The Princess loves soldiers, as I have told you, and knows a great deal about many of the splendid regiments. On this occasion she saluted the Guard of Honour that was drawn up to receive her father. He was wearing the sky-blue service uniform of The Royal Air Force, with whom he fought in the war. Elizabeth is always very proud of her father.

There was not a move in that great Military Tournament which escaped the notice of the blue-eyed, bare-headed child in her little flowered frock. Every so often she would turn to her father and ask a question.

What she liked best about the Tournament that year was the Pageant which brought the Tournament to a close. The soldiers in historical costume presented this pageant, depicting the presentation of the first Prince of Wales to the Welsh people. It was the story of how the English King, Edward I, won over the fierce Welsh Chieftains at the time a Prince was born to Queen Eleanor at Carnarvon

Castle in Wales, on April 25 in 1284. The Welsh-
man had been demanding a native Prince and the
King promised them that their next King would be
from Wales. When a son was born to the Queen
in this old Welsh Castle, King Edward ordered all
the Welsh Chieftains to gather outside the castle.
Then, carrying his infant son before them on his
battle shield, he said, in broken Welsh, "Eich Dyn,"
which meant, "Your Man!"

There was a story to tell Margaret Rose!

That year The Princess Elizabeth went with her
grandmother, the Queen, and her mother, the Duchess
of York, to see the Trooping of the Colour. This is
the most magnificent ceremony in the British Army,
and is carried out on the King's Birthday each year,
in the Horse Guards' parade in honour of His
Majesty.

The Princess thought she had never seen anything
so wonderful as the Trooping of the Colour by the
Grenadier Guards, with all the Guards' Regiments
on parade to honour their King. His Majesty,
seated on his favourite charger, took the salute.
Behind her Royal grandfather were her father, in
the uniform of an Air Vice-Marshal of the Royal
Air Force, and her three uncles.

The Duchess of York, with The Princess Elizabeth,
joined the Queen at the window of the Levee Room

to watch the ceremony. As the King rode down the
Mall to the Horse Guards' Parade, they could hear
the cheers of the thousands of his subjects as they
wished him Many Happy Returns of this Day, and
shouted to him as he rode past, "God bless you,
Sir."

The Princess Elizabeth, who by this time was a very
keen little horsewoman, became very much excited
toward the close of the ceremony, when her uncle
Prince Henry, Duke of Gloucester, got into diffi-
culties with his charger. The horse took fright at
the noise of the massed bands of the Guards Regiments and plunged, reared, and kicked his way across
the parade ground. But the Duke, who is an active
cavalry officer, displayed masterful horsemanship and
finally quieted the animal.

There was another exciting hour in the nursery
when The Princess Elizabeth returned home. It was
such a task to remember everything, and Margaret
Rose expected her not to forget a single detail.

But now, you know, the two Princesses go hand in
hand to the Trooping of the Colour, and to the Royal
Tournament, and to the Aldershot Tattoo and to a
hundred and one ceremonies where many people go,
hoping to see the two sisters.

There are many things Elizabeth likes to do very
much and reading is one of them. Her favourite

The Princess Elizabeth and her grandmother, Queen Mary, visit
Bekonscot model village

The Princess Elizabeth rides with her father in Windsor Park

book, by the way, is *Alice in Wonderland.* The
Princess likes meeting great authors. One day Sir
James Barrie came to visit them at their home.
It was sixteen years since Sir James had written a
play. While he was there, Margaret Rose asked
Sir James if he wouldn't write a play about "David."

Now, good Sir James did not know that little
Margaret Rose's favourite Bible story was that of
David and Goliath. He thought that the Princess
might be referring to her Uncle David, who was then
as you know, Prince of Wales. It was a rather
embarrassing moment for the famous man of letters.

But Elizabeth came to his rescue.

"My sister means the story of David and Goliath,
Sir James," she explained.

"Now, that might be a good idea," said Sir James,
shaking his wise head thoughtfully.

After he had gone home, the more he thought of
the idea, the better he liked it. So he wrote the
play we now know as *Boy David,* a very popular and
great play. Sir James wrote to Princess Margaret
Rose, thanking her for the idea and saying that he
would send her a royalty of tuppence. But The
Princess Elizabeth, who as I have told you, always
looks after her little sister, was not quite certain that
tuppence was enough. So she appointed herself
literary agent to Margaret Rose. That was why

Sir James Barrie received a business-like note from The Princess Elizabeth wanting to know if the tuppence was a "one-time payment of royalty or was it to be for each appearance of the play?"

Yes, the sweet motto on Elizabeth's china, "Two for Joy," was indeed well chosen.

XII

A ROYAL WEDDING

WHEN The Princess Elizabeth was eight years old, two very wonderful things happened to her. She was taken by her father and mother to see her first pantomime, and she was allowed to play an important part in Uncle George's wedding, the most Royal wedding the world had seen for more than a quarter of a century.

It was during the first month of the year that The Princess Elizabeth, her toes tingling with excitement, went to the Lyceum Theatre to see the pantomime. It was a lovely pantomime, and what do you think it was called? Why, *Queen of Hearts*, and who could think of a nicer name for this Princess's first pantomime!

Over three thousand English children, with their mothers and fathers, or their nurses, were at the theatre. And you may be sure that three thousand pairs of eyes watched that eight-year-old miss who stood up in the box between the Duke and Duchess of York, her blue eyes bright with excitement.

But the eyes of the others did not worry Elizabeth. She had come to enjoy the pantomime, just as the others had, and enjoy it she did. There came the time when those thousands of children were asked to sing the chorus of a song. At first, as all children are, they were a bit backward in singing. So Elizabeth, whose mother had taught her to sing and enjoy dozens and dozens of old English and Scottish ballads, saved the situation by leading them through the jolly chorus which started:

"We all went up the mountain——"

How Elizabeth did enjoy that! She liked it so much that she leaned out of the box and waved to the comedian, Mr. George Jackley.

"Please, please, could we sing that again? I'm sure we would do better next time if you would only let us," she called to him, when he had walked across the stage and was near enough to hear her. Mr. Jackley will remember as long as he lives how a real little Princess led his three thousand young friends through the lilting chorus for the second time.

Afterwards Elizabeth told Margaret Rose all about it, and the tiny Princess asked her mother if she could go to the pantomime next year.

"Why, certainly, Margaret Rose," said the Duchess.

The happy Royal Family at "The Little House"

And her mother remembered the promise, for next year Elizabeth and Margaret Rose both went to the Lyceum to see *Dick Whittington* and his world-famed cat.

All in all, it was a splendid start for a very happy year. On the day before her birthday, her grandmother, the Queen, as a very special treat, took her to see the smallest village in all the world. It was at Beaconsfield, and believe it or not, was all in the back yard of a Mr. Callingham, a London accountant. Elizabeth thought she had never seen anything quite so adorable! How she would have liked to take it home for Margaret Rose and herself to play with!

Bekonscot, this tiny town was called. There was just room enough to step from one street to another. The town covered a thousand square feet in its owner's garden. It had everything the ideal town should have, from a perfect little railway station as the terminus of a 1,200-foot-long railway system, to a church with a real organ!

That summer was a glorious one for the two small Princesses at Windsor Great Park, and a busy one, too, what with looking after the Little House and their pets. For besides their dogs there were special pet fawns, the baby deer of the park. And then, too, Elizabeth rode every day under the instruction of Mr. Owen, Royal groom to the Duke of York, who, at the end of the summer, pronounced the Princess an accomplished young horsewoman.

But it was in November that the greatest event of all came about, for it was the month before Christmas that the Duke of Kent married his charming Princess Marina, under the great golden dome of Westminster Abbey.

And what a very royal wedding it was! And, thought Elizabeth, quite fitting for her uncle whom she loved very much, and his beautiful Princess who had come from Greece to be his bride.

For weeks and for months not only the Royal Family but the whole of London had been busy preparing for the wedding. So you can readily imagine that when The Princess Elizabeth heard that she and her friend, Lady Mary Cambridge, were to act as bridesmaids, it made her feel very important indeed. There were to be six other bridesmaids.

Elizabeth had seen many brilliant assemblies and noble gatherings before, but never one so completely indescribable as this. She was glad Margaret Rose could go, because she certainly could not have remembered everything this time to tell her sister when it was all over. The King and Queen were there, of course. And Elizabeth had never seen her grandmother look nicer than she did that day, wearing her sable-trimmed silver and blue cloak over a gown of blue. Upon her gown she was wearing the blue sash of the Order of the Garter. How queenly she did look, thought Elizabeth.

Then she saw her father, looking so very handsome in his naval uniform, and her mother with Margaret Rose grasping her hand tightly, go down the long aisle of the Cathedral. She saw her aunt, the Princess Royal, arrive with her two boy cousins dressed in Eton jackets. Then King Haakon and Queen Maud of Norway arrived, followed by King Christian and Queen Alexandra of Denmark, followed in turn by King George of Greece with Prince Paul, the regent of Yugoslavia.

But none of these royal visitors from overseas caused as much excitement as did Margaret Rose, in her plain little white bonnet and coat. Elizabeth noticed that all the great people that filled the Cathedral smiled and whispered to one another when they saw Margaret Rose walking down that long aisle with her mother. She did hope that Margaret Rose would behave herself when she wasn't with her to look after her! In fact she was more worried about Margaret Rose through the whole ceremony than she was about herself. After all, Margaret Rose was such a tiny little sister.

But just then she saw Princess Marina stepping out of her carriage with her father, the Prince

Nicholas of Greece. She knew that now she must pay attention to her own duties. The Princess Elizabeth and Lady Mary Cambridge caught up the long train of the bride, and, to the strains of the "Wedding March" from *Lohengrin* commenced the long, long journey toward the altar, where Prince George and the Prince of Wales waited.

But Elizabeth acted as a little Princess should act. In fact, Uncle David, the Prince of Wales, as best man, was far more nervous. He fumbled for the ring, he hitched at his sword belt, and he ran a finger nervously round his collar at least a thousand times, so it seemed to Elizabeth, during the ceremony. As for Princess Margaret Rose, she did miss her big sister. She had to sit by herself on a stool in front of her mother's chair, and this fact made Elizabeth all the more nervous. But Margaret Rose, thoughtful little person, soon solved that problem by getting up and moving the stool back close to her mother who whispered to her to pull her blue dress down and stop fidgeting. .

Afterwards, in the chapel of Edward the Confessor, little Princess Elizabeth, along with all the other important people, signed the marriage register as witness. I have seen it myself, and the signature "Elizabeth" is quite one of the neatest on the document.

Through the streets, lined with tens of thousands of his father's cheering subjects, drove the handsome young Prince in the uniform of a Lieutenant-Commander of the Royal Navy and his sweet and charming bride. They drove to Buckingham Palace where the wedding breakfast was to be held. Following them were the King and Queen, with a Captain's Guard clattering along behind the Royal carriage.

Outside the Palace, thousands and thousands of people had gathered to wish the Prince and Princess all the happiness in the world. The good King and Queen led them out on the balcony, and that was just what that cheering crowd wanted. At sight of the happy couple they cheered until the icing on the wedding cake all but cracked. And, by the way, it *was* a cake, for it stood nine feet high and weighed nearly half a ton.

Princess Margaret Rose had to be stopped telling the guests that it had been made in Scotland, for, although that was true, even Princesses should not boast too much of the land of their birth.

It had indeed been a wondrous wedding; one that was quite fitting for any Prince and Princess from a fairy story. But Elizabeth confided to her sister in the nursery afterwards that she was not at all sure but that she liked the other wedding in the little Sussex Church just as much. Probably this was because Margaret Rose had not been to the other wedding, or maybe it was just that The Princess Elizabeth wished to remind her sister that this was really the second time she had been a real bridesmaid.

XIII

THE JUBILEE

IF YOU were to ask any little London boys or girls of today what was the most wonderful thing they had ever seen, they would look at you in amazement. And, because they would know by your question that you must have just arrived from Timbuktu, they would reply, "Why, the King's Jubilee!"

Now, for The Princess Elizabeth and for Princess Margaret Rose, the Jubilee was a hundred times more important and a thousand times more wonderful than anything else! For it was really a special birthday party for their dear grandfather and grandmother, a birthday party to which the whole wide world came! The sixth of May, 1935, when The Princess Elizabeth was nine and Princess Margaret Rose five, was the Silver Jubilee Day. Twenty-five years before, on that same day, their grandfather and grandmother had become King and Queen.

I am sure you must all have heard what a wonderful King and Queen, King George and Queen Mary, had been to the people of the Empire. They were not only rulers of the greatest Empire in history, but they were also the best loved lady and gentleman in all the world. Even people who were not their subjects respected them and loved them dearly.

At their Majesty's Silver Jubilee, these millions of peoples were afforded, for the first time, an opportunity to show that love and loyalty. That is why the Jubilee will always be, to The Princess Elizabeth, just as it will be to all British children who lived at that time, one of the very greatest occasions of their lives. Yes, even though they live to be a hundred and one years old.

The people of the Empire prepared for many months for the Jubilee. During the spring months, ships from across the Seven Seas were bringing people by the thousands and tens of thousands just to attend this day of rejoicing. By the time the Jubilee Day itself came round, there was not a spare bed to be found in all London. Not that these happy people worried particularly about that, for they were quite willing to, and did, sleep in the parks, in the squares, and even on the sidewalks, to await the dawning of the great day.

And when it came, God Himself seemed to smile upon the most loved King and Queen in Christendom,

The Princess Elizabeth stoops to peek as she enters St. Paul's
on Jubilee Day

for He rolled back the clouds and flooded the stage with beautiful golden sunshine.

The big event of this Royal birthday party and thanksgiving was the State drive from Buckingham Palace to St. Paul's Cathedral, where King George and Queen Mary went to give thanks before their God. And in the Royal procession to and from the Cathedral were the Royal Family in three other carriages. The first carriage bore the Prince of Wales and his aunt, the Queen of Norway, also the Duke of Gloucester. In the second were the Duke and Duchess of York, and our two little Princesses; and in the third, the Duke and Duchess of Kent.

All along that route, lined every inch of the way with soldiers and sailors—not to guard the King and Queen, but to honour them—it seemed as if the whole of England had gathered. On the Mall and on Constitution Hill great stands of seats had been built from which seventy thousand subjects could watch the Royal procession. But these stands held only a small section of the masses of people who had come from all over England, yes, and from all over the world! Cavalry regiments that came clattering out of the dawn were lost in the crowds, for the people had gathered by the millions long before sun-up.

Elizabeth and Margaret Rose, seated in their carriage facing their father and mother, with two footmen in their gold livery perched on the box behind, were quite sure they had no idea so many, many people ever lived.

Oh, what a drive that was! If it hadn't been for looking after Margaret Rose, Elizabeth was sure she would have stood up on the seat. As it was, after stopping Margaret Rose twice from pointing, she caught herself doing the same embarrassing thing! Two million is a lot of people, but more than that number cheered as they passed on that day of the King's and Queen's special birthday party. Elizabeth's arm ached for days afterwards, for she was waving it and bowing all the way to St. Paul's and back. As for Margaret Rose, well, at times, she waved both her arms, and in such an excited manner that Elizabeth was sure she saw just the suspicion of a smile on the face of one person, at least. He was the Captain of the Royal Horse Guard escort who clattered along beside them, with a drawn sabre, his scarlet helmet plume dancing all the while.

Standing high on the steps leading into the Cathedral while the Royal Family were awaiting the arrival of the King and Queen, Elizabeth could see far out over the crowds on the street, people who looked as if they had been stood on end and fitted together like a gigantic jig-saw puzzle. For the first time she noticed people falling, and ambulance men and police picking them up. It frightened her.

"Look, Mummy, there's a poor lady fallen down over there. Oh, look, there's a soldier just fallen over!"

The poor Princess was almost on the verge of tears when a tall officer stepped forward and saluted.

"It's all right, Your Royal Highness," he whispered to Elizabeth, "they are only fainting and in a few minutes they will be as well as ever. See how well the police and ambulance men are looking after them."

"Oh, thank you so much," said Elizabeth to the smiling officer. "I wouldn't like them to be really ill."

But now the King and Queen were entering the Cathedral and the Royal Family was to follow them.

Once and just once Elizabeth forgot herself. That was when they entered St. Paul's and she stooped down and looked between the Prince of Wales and Queen Maud at the throng inside the Cathedral. Her little heart almost stood still at what she saw!

Into that stately Cathedral was crowded the great of a whole Empire—a carpet of the richest colours known to man, woven into one human assembly. There were the gold and scarlet cloth of Royalty; the scarlet and blue of the Navy, the Army, and

Air Force and the State, mingled with the rich dress of the Princes of India; the gold encrusted Court dress of Statesmen from all the King's Dominions beyond the Seas; of foreign Ambassadors, and the sombre civilian dress of the great men of letters and the sciences, mingled with the rustling of silks worn by their ladies.

Never will these two little Princesses, nor any of those in St. Paul's that day, ever forget the magnificence and splendour of that company of the great.

The King and Queen were seated directly below the pulpit and behind their faldstools. On a cushion on top of the high stool in front of His Majesty the King, rested his Field Marshal's baton. On a table in front was the pearl-hilted Sword of the City of London, which had been surrendered to him at the City Boundary. A shaft of sunlight entering from above through the lofty windows of the Nave bathed in gold the spot under the Great Dome where the King and Queen sat.

The Princess Elizabeth sat on a chair beside her mother, directly behind the King. In front of her on a stool was Princess Margaret Rose.

That afternoon the whole of the Royal Family gathered at Buckingham Palace, and from the balcony, the King and Queen acknowledged the cheers of over two hundred thousand people massed below.

(0)

His Majesty, King George VI, and his eldest daughter, The
Princess Elizabeth, Heir Presumptive

Elizabeth was not tall enough to wave over the draped balustrade or balcony. But Grandfather and Grandmother held Margaret Rose up several times until her two cousins, the Lascelles children, ran inside the Palace and carried a chair out for the wee Princess to stand upon.

The Jubilee celebrations were not to be completed on this one day, for they lasted for weeks and weeks, with all the important buildings of old London bright by night under the constant white glare of floodlights. I am afraid it was very, very late before The Princess Elizabeth and Princess Margaret Rose went to sleep on the night of Jubilee Day. The cheering, shouting, good-natured throngs that had come to the Good King's very special birthday party lasted almost the whole night through. For the first time, Elizabeth saw tears in the eyes of her kind grandfather. They were tears of gratitude!

It was in August of that year that Elizabeth and Margaret Rose with their father and mother journeyed to Glamis Castle, to holiday with their Scottish grandfather and grandmother, the Earl and Countess of Strathmore.

Their holiday in Scotland each year was a great event to these two little sisters, for even though they did worry the grown-ups a little with their tree climbing and other escapades, it really was a

7

wonderful treat to visit their mother's grand old home in the Highlands.

But this year, particularly for Elizabeth, the visit to Glamis Castle was even more romantic and interesting than usual. For it so happened that the Black Watch, the most famous Highland Regiment of the British Army, was in camp at Montrose, and was to receive new Colours from the hands of the Duchess of York. Elizabeth knew that the Colours of such a regiment are very precious indeed. They are known as representing the soul of the regiment. On the regimental Colour is borne the name of each and every battle honour that the regiment has won on the field. Because they represent not only the valiant deeds of the regiment but also those members of the regiment who, through their sacrifice had made such victories possible, all men bare their heads when the Colours are carried past.

Elizabeth and Margaret Rose stood upon the saluting base with their father and mother when that great regiment marched past with its new Colours. Kilts swinging, white spats lifting and falling to the lilt of the pipes! Four of Elizabeth's Scottish uncles had gone marching off to the war with this splendid regiment; Patrick, John, Michael, and Fergus. She never knew her Uncle Fergus for he, Major Fergus Bowes-Lyon, was killed at the head

of his company at Loos in 1915. And, too, her
Uncle Michael had been severely wounded and spent
many dread years in a prison camp and did not
return until the end of the war. Elizabeth knew
that this uncle had given up his turn to leave the
stark prison camp and go to Holland, in favour of a
more badly wounded brother officer.

You can imagine just how Elizabeth felt on the
day when her Scottish mother presented those new
and glorious Colours to the Black Watch. She was
thinking of her Uncle Fergus whom she had often
wished she had known.

Jubilee Year had a wonderful ending for the two
Princesses, for it was in November of that year that
their soldier uncle, Prince Henry, Duke of Gloucester,
married a charming Scottish lady. She was Lady
Alice Montague-Douglas-Scott, daughter of the Duke
of Buccleuch, a great Scottish nobleman, whose title
went as far back in Scots history as did that of
the Duchess of York's family. Lady Alice is
a delightful person, who loves horses as much as
Elizabeth did. She was always a great favourite
with these two little Princesses of York.

Elizabeth and Margaret Rose were bridesmaids at
the wedding. It was held in the scarlet and gold
Royal Chapel in the Palace. After the ceremony
the Prince of Wales, who was again best man, led

the Princesses in a well-planned raid as the newly married Duke and Duchess were leaving the Palace in their carriage.   They showered the laughing Duke and Duchess with rose petals and confetti as they ran beside the carriage until it reached the Palace gates.

XIV

HIS MAJESTY'S LAST COURT

CHRISTMAS to the two little Princesses always
meant Sandringham, the country residence of
their grandfather, for here the Royal grandchildren
always gathered for a jolly family Christmas party.

At Sandringham in beautiful Norfolk, the Christmas party of the Royal Family had become famous
throughout the Empire. People on Christmas Day,
not only in England, but in Africa, Canada, Australia, and India, always thought of the Good King
presiding over a jolly Christmas gathering of his
children, now grown up, and his grandchildren.
Indeed, the children of the Empire were in one sense,
able to join in the family circle at Sandringham
when the King's kindly voice carried to them all a
special Christmas message over the radio.

"My words will be very simple, but spoken from
the heart on this family festival of Christmas," the
King had said on this Christmas Day to the people
of his Empire. "Once again as I close I send to
you all, and not the least to the children who may

be listening to me, my truest Christmas wishes, and those of my dear wife, my children, and my grandchildren who are with me today. I add the heartfelt prayer that, wherever you are, God may bless and keep you always."

This was the King's wish and prayer as he spoke to his subjects the world over. Always, on Christmas, he sent a special message to the children.

So this happy Christmas at Sandringham passed for The Princess Elizabeth and Princess Margaret Rose. It had been a Christmas of exciting presents to all the family and to every member of the household down to the youngest and most humble servant—a Christmas of a bright shining tree that the King lighted by the touch of a magic electric button. Above all, it had been a happy, happy Christmas with Grandfather.

Elizabeth's Royal grandfather had not been in the best of health but he did, however, manage to get in a few days' good shooting, of which he was very fond. And almost every day he rode Jock, his faithful old white pony, or walked through the grounds and village. But the little Princesses were not surprised, though, of course, they were very sorry when they heard that Grandfather had a cold and had to stay in bed. It was just the sort of weather for colds—rain one day and sleet the next—and they hoped that in a day or so Grandfather would be better. For Christmas holidays were not the same without him, his quick smile, and his little jokes.

But the King did not get better. As the days passed, the worried manners of the grown-ups made Elizabeth very unhappy and very much afraid. Officers of State were rushing backward and forward from London, and her uncle, the Prince of Wales, who had returned to London after Christmas Day, quickly came back to Sandringham.

On Saturday morning it snowed in Norfolk, and the two little Princesses played all morning amid the white flakes. But at luncheon their mother told them that this afternoon they must both leave and go back to White Lodge in Windsor Park. No, Father and Mummy would not go with them, but would stay to look after Grandfather.

"The Princess Elizabeth of York and Princess Margaret of York have left Sandringham. Their Majesties' other guests have also left. The Princess Royal arrived today."

Thus read the brief Court Circular of that day. Just as it had made Elizabeth and Margaret Rose who wanted to stay with their grandfather very unhappy, so the Court Circular made the whole of the Empire afraid. You see, the people of the Empire knew that it must be a very serious thing indeed that took the two Princesses away from Sandringham on their Christmas holidays.

On Tuesday morning Elizabeth awoke early in the nursery at the Royal Lodge. What was that? It was a bell tolling slowly, very slowly. The whole house was hushed. She looked out the window. Everything was very still and quiet except for the tolling bell. When nurse came in, Elizabeth could see that she had been crying.

The King was dead. Dear, kind Grandfather, the greatest gentleman she had ever known had returned to God, "by whom Kings and Queens do reign."

This broken-hearted little girl in her nursery began to realize the meaning of it all. There would be no more Christmases at Sandringham, nor any other days, with Grandfather.

They brought the body of the King back from his beloved country home. In historic Westminster Hall he rested in State until the Kings and Ambassadors could gather to bid him farewell.

It was the sorrowing Queen who took Elizabeth to this last court of her grandfather at the Great Hall one evening. They entered through a private doorway and stood side by side, unrecognized, as thousands of the departed King's subjects passed before him, many weeping. The Princess had never thought that anything so majestic existed as this

Last Court of her Royal grandfather. Out along the Thames embankment the people gathered, more than twenty abreast in a winding queue that trailed for three miles.

Silently Elizabeth and the Queen stood and watched the people and the changing of the Guard. For around the last Throne of her grandfather stood three Gentlemen-at-Arms, the long white swan's feathers of their tall helmets lifting with each opening and closing of the doors. Below them, with heads bent over the hilts of their naked swords, stood four officers of the Life Guards in full dress uniform, their breast plates and polished jack boots reflecting the light of the candles. At the hour of midnight, Elizabeth's three uncles and her father took over that honoured Last Guard duty.

Elizabeth was glad, afterwards, that the Queen had taken her to see that Last Court, where humble and rich alike came side by side to pay their respects to a great and good King.

It was on Tuesday morning of the next week that they carried the King's body from Westminster Hall and bore it to Windsor Castle Chapel. It had been raining all night and the flags at half-mast hung tightly to their poles. All night long, people had been gathering that they might honour their dead King on his last journey from London. Over two million people came to the huge city by train. Among them were five Kings and scores of Princes and Ambassadors from other countries.

Slowly the procession, headed by the massed bands of the Guards, moved towards Paddington Station. As the gun-carriage, pulled by one hundred forty seamen of the Royal Navy, moved off, the first of a long artillery salute was fired in Hyde Park. At each firing of the minute guns, the windows rattled at 145, Piccadilly. A little girl, bareheaded, stood on the balcony of that house, and watched her dear grandfather leave London. Just as he passed below, Princess Margaret Rose made a beautiful little curtsey, her own farewell to Grandfather.

At Paddington Station, The Princess Elizabeth waited the long procession. Poor Princess! She looked very white in her tight-fitting black beret and coat. With her mother she journeyed to Windsor Castle and, from the choir under the Knight's Banners, she saw her grandfather placed to rest in peace with his honoured forefathers.

Poor, dear Grandfather! As she left the Chapel, Elizabeth noticed that the air was filled with fragrance and that the lawns of Windsor had blossomed into the most beautiful of flowers. These more than five thousand individual floral tributes from Kings and commoners, had been sent to her grandfather.

Amid this rich carpet of flowers were great wreaths from Governments and Princes that must have cost a king's ransom.   Yet of all these, Elizabeth will remember most outstandingly one: a wee bunch of garden flowers with a note on which some child had written, "Dear King."   You see, she knew that would have made her dear grandfather very, very happy, for he loved all little children.

And now Uncle David was King.   Elizabeth thought the young King looked terribly lonely as if, as he walked, the whole world were pressing upon him.

XV

ABDICATION AND PROCLAMATION

NOW, it may seem very strange to you and hard to understand, but you will have to believe me when I tell you that The Princess Elizabeth was the only person in all England, besides her sister, who did not know of the great crisis which the Empire faced a few weeks before Christmas of 1936.

Yet, it was so, and even though the crisis concerned Kind Edward, her own favourite uncle with the winning smile and the understanding heart, her own dear grandmother and her father and mother (who were, after all, most vitally concerned), the two little Princesses were not told of the grave and dark days until the first ray of sunlight came sweeping out of the storm clouds.

Elizabeth knew that something very, very serious was being faced by the grown-up world. More great men came to see her father during the week than in a whole year, and she noticed that they were all quite grave and worried. Then, too, Father was driving off to visit the King, his brother, and his mother at all hours of the day and night. And such a roar of despatch riders and motorcycles as she had never heard before.

Of course she asked questions! First she asked Mother and Father, then Nannie, and then her governess. But they all were silent, except for the promise that tomorrow she might know. But tomorrow did not come for days and days.

It was the morning of the three hundred and twenty-fifth day of King Edward's reign that the Duchess of York interrupted the lesson hour to tell Elizabeth. The King had abdicated! Her Uncle David was going away on a holiday. Her own dear father was to be King and her beloved mother, Queen.

It was, to be sure, very difficult for a little girl to understand. She was very, very sorry that her favourite uncle was going away on a long holiday and with Christmas just a few days away, too! She had always thought of her Uncle David as a knight-errant in shining armour like the story-book knights of King Arthur's Court. She knew he had been a truly mighty prince, the most beloved Prince of Wales England had ever had, just as her grand-father had been the most beloved King.

Elizabeth knew that her father and mother would come to be a great king and queen just as her dear grandfather and grandmother had been. She was not at all certain that she and Margaret Rose would like moving into Buckingham Palace, for after all, 145, Piccadilly was their home with little friends living close by. Yet it would mean Christmas at Sandringham again and her mother promised her that they would all go to Sandringham this very Christmas and that she might invite Lady Mary Cambridge to stay with her for the Christmas holidays.

The next day was a busy one for her father, the King, with great statesmen coming and going all the morning, and long hours in his study with his Secretary, Admiral Sir Basil Brook. Elizabeth and Margaret Rose were allowed to play in the garden, at a thrilling game of hide-and-seek, while thousands gathered in front of the new King's home. Her Scottish grandmother, the Countess of Strathmore, came to visit the Queen, and Elizabeth walked with her grandmother to the gate where she kissed her good-bye.

The next morning King George left to go to the Throne Room of St. James's Palace. Elizabeth thought her father had never looked so handsome as on this day when, in the blue and gold uniform of an Admiral of the Fleet, he went to the great golden Throne Room. Here the Lords of his Privy Council were to offer their allegiance to a new King-Emperor.

How delighted she and Margaret Rose were when the Queen said they might go with their father in the afternoon to hear the Proclamation from St. James's Palace, for all Kings are proclaimed King-Emperor in this beautiful old ceremony. The Queen, because of a bad cold, could not go with her two daughters. At three o'clock they left 145, Piccadilly with the King and drove down Constitution Hill. Thousands and tens of thousands cheered them on their way. The King smiled and lifted his hat while the two Princesses waved to these good people who were now their father's subjects.

Long before three o'clock, thousands of men, women, and children had gathered about St. James's to hear the new King proclaimed with old-world pageantry. They surged from Trafalgar Square and swarmed through Admiralty Arch, on to the Mall. Although over thirteen regiments of soldiers and hundreds of policemen were on duty for the Proclamation, a squadron of the Royal Horse Guards had to be pressed into duty to help keep the roadways cleared.

The King and his two little daughters drove amid a storm of cheers to Marlborough House, where good Queen Mary lives. Here, with the Queen-Mother, they watched the ceremony from a tall window overlooking the Friary Court.

In the court itself they could see the King's Company of the Guards drawn up in line with the King's Colour facing the balcony, and on its flank the regimental band. An escort of the Royal Horse Guards, with their long scarlet capes, filled Marlborough Gate with martial colour.

As the clock in the Tower above struck three, four Royal trumpeters in scarlet and gold led the way on to the court balcony. They were followed by the Heralds and the Officers of Arms, all habited in their gorgeous tabards that bear the Arms of England.

Sir Gerald Wollaston, in a strong, clear voice, sent the words of the Proclamation over the heads of the throng that stood bareheaded.

"— is now become our only lawful and rightful Liege Lord George the Sixth, by the Grace of God, of Great Britain, Ireland, and the British Dominions Beyond the Seas, King, Defender of the Faith, Emperor of India: To whom we do acknowledge all Faith and constant Obedience, with all hearty and humble affection, beseeching God, by whom all Kings and Queens do reign, to bless the Royal Prince George the Sixth with long and happy years to reign over us."

The Garter King of Arms sprang to attention and shouted, "Long live the King!" Ten thousand

Historic Glamis Castle.   The Princesses and their mother leave the Castle for a Highland visit

tongues echoed it, and with a mighty shout sent it up to the window where the King stood with his mother and his two small daughters. The windows shook. That was the artillery salute honouring a new and loved King at the Tower of London and in Hyde Park.

And so now, in very fact, was Elizabeth's kind father, King and Emperor over a quarter of the world, with 486,000,000 loyal subjects in the greatest Empire the world has ever known. An Empire, which Elizabeth will most probably some day rule herself. As the King-Emperor and the two little Princesses drove back to their home, the people stormed the car and it was only with difficulty that the police made way for it, for you see fifty thousand people had known they would be driving home and had got there before them.

The two Princesses, excited beyond words, ran quickly up the steps ahead of their father. The Princess Elizabeth, laughing, turned and waved a tiny handkerchief to all her father's good subjects and Princess Margaret jumped up and down and forgot to wave altogether.

Then all three entered their home where they were to join the Queen for tea.

XVI

CHRISTMAS AT SANDRINGHAM

THE story of Christmas at Sandringham is one of the very happiest in the lives of the two little Princesses. It is not a story of a King-Emperor or of a golden court but of a great English gentleman and his lady and how they and their children choose to spend the most joyful days of the year.

To Elizabeth and Margaret Rose these Christmas holidays at Sandringham are days set apart. They bring gay laughter and jolly games, roaring log fires, holly and mistletoe, a glorious Christmas tree, with hundreds of lights that sparkle like so many stars. Regiments of puddings all sprouting holly on top and surrounded by dancing blue fingers of flame. The excitement of surprises that come bundled in snowy white paper, held tight with red ribbons. And best of all, the surprises that they have for others.

Weeks before Christmas The Princess Elizabeth is hard at work with a busy needle making presents with her own hands. With the departure for Sandringham, it is no longer necessary when Mother or Father or Grandmother pay a visit to the nursery to hide her handiwork hurriedly behind her back. Then there are the presents which Elizabeth and Margaret Rose themselves buy after weeks and months of saving pocket money. And, oh, how the pocket money does fly away at Christmas time!

It was four days before Christmas and but eleven days after her father had become King-Emperor that the Royal Family left for Sandringham by the special Royal Express. True, Elizabeth had ridden in the Royal train before, but that was when her grandfather had been King. But, exciting though it was to ride in her Royal father's special train for the first time and watch the snow-flecked country-side go slipping past as they speeded toward the beautiful county of Norfolk, it was much more important, so the Princess thought, to get to Sandringham as fast as the train could get them there.

Wolferton is a small Norfolk town of but a few hundred people, and Wolferton Station is really little better than a siding. No matter; the whole countryside waited there that day to welcome their King and Queen and the two little Princesses, and even though the Royal train was five minutes ahead of time, these good Norfolk country folk were waiting long before, many of them having walked miles and miles.　And how they did cheer when the King and Queen, followed by the two children wearing long tweed coats, Elizabeth without a hat, stepped from the train.

At Sandringham village, the cottagers lined the road to welcome them.　But to these villagers, Elizabeth's father and mother were not only King and Queen, they were their very own "Squire" and his lady.

"The new Squire" they called the King, for, you see, Elizabeth's beloved grandfather had been the good, kind Squire to them for so many, many years.

As the car rolled along over the wooded roads that are a part of the Sandringham estate, Bob, Queen Mary's Cairn terrier, who had been an excited member of the party since they left London, barked noisily and pressed his black nose to the window when he caught sight of many dogs out for a run on the lawns.　The two Princesses lowered the windows of the car and called to the dogs.　There were six Clumber Spaniels and four Labrador Retrievers, all wise hunting dogs from the Sandringham kennels. What wonderful playfellows they were for two little girls on their Christmas holidays!

Sandringham House, the King's country home where the two Princesses will spend Christmas for many, many years to come, is indeed a beautiful house.　It is Elizabethan in design, with great open

Princess Elizabeth shaking hands with the Duke of Norfolk, the
Earl Marshall, who received her at the Coronation

leaded windows and walls covered with ivy and vines. It stands in a wooded park of two hundred acres and faces the most beautiful lake you could ever hope to see. Altogether, Sandringham is an estate of over seven thousand acres, with rolling farm lands, quaint, old-fashioned village cottages and copses and woods, marshes and waterlands that teem with wild fowl and game. The old Squire, Elizabeth's grandfather, was the best shot in all England, perhaps we should say in all Europe, and it was here that he spent his happiest hours, with his favourite gun and his hunting dogs.

Every room of the great house had been decorated for Christmas. For days, woodsmen had been cutting holly and mistletoe on the estate, and when the two little girls were safely asleep, servants worked until long past the hour of midnight decorating the nursery, with the hope that it would delight the two Princesses when they awoke. They were not disappointed. When the first grey dawn came in through the leaded windows from the grey sea, gasps of delight came from two excited children.

You may be sure that the two days before Christmas were quite the busiest that Elizabeth had ever known. Her father, the King, spent all of the first day visiting tenants and discussing farm problems and garden work with the staff of the estate. In the great house itself, her mother, the Queen, and her grandmother were busy superintending the last-minute Christmas preparations.

I doubt very much if there is a happier place than Sandringham House at Christmas, or in fact, a busier place in the world than the kitchen there. No less than six bullocks had been cut up to provide roast beef, and hundreds of Norfolk turkeys, and there are none finer, prepared for the great day to come, not to mention dozens and dozens of plum puddings and mince pies.

Christmas Eve was breath-taking! The Princesses helped the King and Queen and their Royal grandmother to distribute great joints of beef, turkeys, and plum puddings to tenants and workers on the estate, for all at Sandringham must share in Christmas fare.

Earlier in the day the Princess Elizabeth and Princess Margaret Rose had helped Queen Mary with the presents which Her Majesty, the Queen Mother, gave to all pensioners on the estate and to all the school children of the district.

"It was the night before Christmas ———." And, while two Princesses dreamed of tomorrow, the telephones at Sandringham House rang cheerily just before midnight. It was their uncle, H.R.H. Prince Edward, Duke of Windsor, calling from an historic castle in far-off Austria. In the morning

The Princess Elizabeth felt very disappointed that Uncle David should have telephoned after bedtime. But he called up again on Christmas Day, so her favourite uncle was quite forgiven.

The two Princesses were out of bed with a bound on Christmas morning and over to the nursery fire-place, where two stockings bulged with good things. Near by, and much too large to go in the stockings, stood two parcels whose wrappings bore Austrian stamps—a skittle-board game for each of them, sent by the Duke of Windsor.

All too soon for the Princesses came time to dress for church. With the King and Queen, the Princess Alice, the Duke of Athlone, the Duke and Duchess of Gloucester, and Lady Mary Cambridge, they walked through the grounds to quaint Sandringham Church for Christmas morning service. At the top of their voices the Princess Elizabeth and Princess Margaret Rose sang "Hark, the Herald Angels Sing," and "O Come all ye Faithful."

After church, like so many millions of other children, the two Princesses sat down with the family for Christmas dinner of roast beef and tur-key, plum pudding and mince pie. Grandmother was seated at the head of the happy family table.

Then came the great moment when the King led the way into the ballroom, with the two children dancing by his side. What do you think was there? Why, the grandest Christmas tree of all, over thirty feet high and sparkling with stars and lights all different shades and colours. Elizabeth and Margaret Rose jumped up and down with glee as their father pressed the button which set the tree glowing and twinkling with all its many lights. Presents for all were piled around the tree like drifted snow. Yes, presents for all the household, from the youngest scullery maid to the oldest retainer, and the two Princesses, very busy little persons indeed, handed them out to the happy people of Sandringham House.

Later, it was back to the nursery to put on party frocks, then downstairs again to join the family in the drawing room for tea, with Christmas cake covered with silvery icing and with its hidden charms.

At nine o'clock that night, two very tired children, but so happy that all the toy animals seemed to sing with glee, went to their beds, planning for tomorrow until heavy eyelids closed in contentment.

Such is Sandringham at Christmas time! A kingdom of happiness and joy over which two little girls reign and will reign for years to come.

Yes, if you were to ask the Princess Elizabeth which of her many titles she liked the best, I know she would reply, "Why, daughter of the Squire of Sandringham!"

XVII

ELIZABETH OF YORK

B Y THE time The Princess Elizabeth approached
her eleventh birthday, she was indeed a very
remarkable little girl. She was rapidly becoming
fitted, although she did not know it, for the great
task which was coming nearer to her. Indeed, even
if she were not a Princess of York, she would still
be a very clever and glamorous young lady in her
own right.

I would say that Elizabeth was, first of all, a
studious girl, for she loved to learn things. Whether
it is helping her father at his favourite hobby of
building wireless sets, or in her classroom studying,
she seems to take a delight in learning things.

There is nothing that delights the Princess more
than reading, and she loves to spend any spare half
hour in her busy days with a favourite new book.

You might imagine that Elizabeth, by this descrip-
tion, was a little bookworm, always ready to shrink
behind a pair of spectacles and printed pages.
Nothing is further from the truth, and I hope Her

Royal Highness will forgive me, but I must tell you that at heart she has in the past been somewhat of a "tomboy." Climbing trees and riding bicycles has always been a particular interest of hers. Her favourite trick just at present is to ride her bicycle without either hand on the handlebars, a trick she learned on the gravel paths of her garden, despite many a hard fall into the shrubbery.

Not only is she studious but she is also a very much out-of-doors girl, and in sports she is far above the average. The Princess Elizabeth has one of the best "seats" in a saddle and the nicest "hands" you could possibly hope to see. When in the country at the Royal Lodge, she rides every day and is considered an excellent horsewoman. Her father's gift to her on her last birthday was a beautiful saddle horse. She is also a good swimmer and, during the winter, is to be found daily in the spacious tank of the famous Bath Club, where her "Uncle David" played squash almost every day to keep in form.

If you were to visit the Princess at her home for tea, you would not be allowed to leave before seeing something that she prizes above everything else that is her very own. What do you suppose it is? Why, a medal that she won all by herself, a medal given her at the Bath Club because she was the best swimmer and diver of her age. And who can blame Elizabeth for showing it to all her special friends?

As far as her lessons are concerned, the Princess likes geography and history best of all, and arithmetic and French the least. Miss Crawford, her visiting French governess, aided by the fact that her mother and father insisted on French conversation as much as possible, has helped overcome her dislike for the language. Now she not only talks and recites in excellent French, but also sings in that language. She can also sew beautifully and can cook very well. Indeed, she baked and iced a cake herself and sent it to an exhibition of children's work the very week that her father became king. You can be sure it was greatly admired by children and grown-ups alike. Dancing seems to come naturally to her, for both her father and mother are excellent on the ballroom floor. Under the teaching of her Dancing Governess, Miss Vacani, she has learned not only ballroom dancing, but the most intricate Scottish dances and reels as well. But there is nothing The Princess Elizabeth enjoys more than tap-dancing as taught her by Miss Vacani. Very often the little Princess can be found in the nursery teaching her grown-up visitors just how a good tap-dancer ought to perform.

Both the princesses, and more particularly The Princess Elizabeth, love music, and each has a

miniature piano of her own.   The Princess Elizabeth
has a sweet voice and from her mother has learned to
sing old English and Scottish ballads beautifully.
Often the two sisters go to the Countess of Cavan's
house where they join a music class made up of the
children who are their particular friends.

The Princess Elizabeth has many charming little
friends.   I have already told you that one of her
closest friends is Lady Mary Cambridge, who is
but two years older than the Princess and is a
daughter of the Marquis of Cambridge.   Another
close friend is tiny Miss Sonia Hodgson who lives on
Upper Brook Street.   Sonia's father is the Queen's
doctor.   Still another friend is Lady Mary Elizabeth Stewart, daughter of the Marquess of
Londonderry.   She is the same age as Lady
Mary Cambridge.

Elizabeth delights in playing games with her
friends and at present games of "make-believe" are
the favourites.   One afternoon they play circus,
with the children taking the part of various animals
in the show.   Each has to do tricks just as the
lions and the tigers, the elephants and the ponies
do in a real circus.   The next afternoon the children
are "ponies" and are "broken" and taught to jump,
with grown-ups taking the part of the owners and
the grooms.

Sandringham, where The Princess Elizabeth spends Christmas holidays

A lady whom I know who often used to have tea with the two girls told me that one particular afternoon when she was visiting the nursery, The Princess Elizabeth and Princess Margaret Rose had a special surprise for her. They played the "Pied Piper" for her, The Princess Elizabeth taking the part of the Pied Piper and Margaret Rose the crippled child of the play.

Musical chairs and charades, a game in which one of the children acts a word and the others guess it, are two favourite pastimes of the two children. And we must not forget hide-and-seek. Hide-and-seek as played by The Princess Elizabeth and her sister in the garden at 145, Piccadilly is a real game, with all sorts of wonderful places to hide. That makes the game almost as exciting as big-game hunting.

Of course, like all small girls of her age, The Princess Elizabeth likes pretty clothes and always helps her mother choose them. She very often wears a wool frock in the winter or a tweed skirt and cardigan, over which she wears a tweed coat. She would rather go out bareheaded, her fair hair free to the wind, than to wear a hat.

I am afraid that when I write about The Princess Elizabeth, her clothes, and her shopping, many of my young readers will perhaps think of her as having all the money she wants to buy the things she likes.   As a matter of fact, The Princess Elizabeth is given a shilling a week as spending money.   This allowance, which amounts to about twenty-five cents, is given her by her mother, the Queen, each month.   And she must bank it, for, as you know, there are a thousand and one ways for a little girl to spend twenty-five cents, and if it were not put in the bank, by the time spring came, there would not be a penny left with which to buy seeds and plants for her garden.

Princess Margaret Rose is not yet considered old enough to have even a shilling a week of her very own.

Always since they were very, very tiny girls, Elizabeth and Margaret Rose have been brought up to love animals.   Today they have many pets.   Besides their ponies there are, first of all, the family dogs. There are eight in all, and, like all English dogs, they are very much members of the family and have the run of the house.   Of course, Elizabeth loves them all, for the two Princesses are responsible for the grooming and care of them.   But her very own are Dookie and Jane, the mischievous reddish brown Pembrokeshire Corgis, with the friendliest black muzzles.

Besides Jane and Dookie, the two sisters have their own pet fawns in the Royal deer herd at

Windsor Great Park which they visit daily when the
family is staying at the Royal Lodge. The Lodge,
their unpretentious country home, is only three miles
from Fort Belvedere, where Elizabeth used to go so
often to admire her Uncle David's garden. You
see, she is very fond of flowers and of gardening
herself.

Now, I am sure you are at a loss to know how
these two very busy Princesses manage to find time
to learn so much and do so much. Well, I will take
you to 145, Piccadilly for an average day, as Elizabeth follows the clock round.

7.30.   The Princess Elizabeth gets up, bathes,
and dresses.

8.30.   Breakfast time in the nursery with Princess
Margaret Rose. They usually have ce-
real, fish, or eggs. Then they have prayers
with Mother and Father, or if they are
away, with Nannie in the nursery.

10.00.   Lessons begin with their governess, but
before lessons there is time to write a
few letters or read a favourite book.

12.00.   There is time for a short play in the garden
before luncheon.

12.45.   Luncheon, usually chicken and vegetables
and a sweet. After luncheon, shopping
with Mother or perhaps a visit to Grand-

mother. On certain days, dancing and music lessons, and often tea with their friends in the nursery. They have bread and butter and jam, homemade cakes, often baked by Elizabeth, and tea or chocolate. This is the usual fare.

5.00.   The best hour of the day for it is spent with Father and Mother. Often a family musical hour with Mother at the piano.

7.00.   A light supper in the nursery and a final reading of a favourite book.

8.00.   Bath and then bed.

And you may be sure that they are two very, very tired little Princesses who lay their heads upon the pillow to set sail for dreamland.